FOOTBALL IS BETTER WITH FANS

FOOTBALL IS BETTER WITH FANS

DEVOTION AND EMOTION.
CHEERS AND BEERS.

TONY RICKSON

First published by Pitch Publishing, 2021

Pitch Publishing
A2 Yeoman Gate
Yeoman Way
Worthing
Sussex
BN13 3QZ
www.pitchpublishing.co.uk
info@pitchpublishing.co.uk

A CIP catalogue record is available for this book
from the British Library.

ISBN 978 1 80150 000 5

Typesetting and origination by Pitch Publishing
Printed and bound in India by Replika Press Pvt. Ltd.

Contents

1

Super shambles: No one likes us

IT'S GREAT fun being a football fan. The whole matchday experience starts with the anticipation on the morning of the game; the slightly tense and nervy feeling of butterflies in the stomach. Then there's the important choice of the right clothes to wear and planning the journey to the ground. It's about meeting up with friends for a pie and a pint, walking the last bit before going inside the stadium, and getting a first breathtaking glimpse of the magically green grass. Then there's work to be done. Clapping the players as they come out to warm up and cheering them all over again when they emerge for the match itself. And the following 90 minutes of breathless, heartwarming action. The singing, the chanting, the drama, the excitement, the celebrations, the passion. Being a part of it; the warm tingle of camaraderie. Win, lose or draw, enough memories to see you through the whole of the following week.

Of course, nothing's ever perfect and as we got stuck into the 21st century there was the odd niggle. The game itself was different from how it used to be, many complained. Cleverer perhaps, and certainly more tactical, but perhaps lacking the bite and fury of days gone by. New stadiums were far safer, but that was another moan – they lack the atmosphere and familiarity of the old ones they replaced. The cost of watching a match had soared, as had the prices of merchandise in the club shop, as well as buying in the digital channels required to see all the top games on TV. Many clubs, particularly at the top of the English game, had foreign owners, giving the fans a sense of being distanced from the feeling of 'we're all in this together'. To the absentee owners it was a business; to the fans it was a passion. Diehard fans who'd supported the club man and boy, through thick and thin, felt resentful sitting next to a one-off glory-hunter fan who had no local roots and was there for a day out once a year.

And, in the Premier League at least, there was VAR, throwing up controversial, even shocking, decisions. Fans at the match were excluded from what was happening as vital decisions were taken from far away based on slow-motion replays which often distorted the action. Other sports had found ways around explaining what was going on to those who'd paid to be in the stadium, but football hadn't. The whole system meant the huge joy of goal celebrations often went out of the window as an often endless amount of time was needed to check and recheck ludicrously marginal decisions.

All valid reasons for a supporter to complain that things weren't how they used to be. Mind you, one fan remembered in a Facebook post how he was given a lecture by a fellow supporter about how good it had been watching football 20 years earlier. And that conversation had taken place back in 1987!

Suddenly, and dramatically, it swiftly turned a whole lot worse. The coronavirus pandemic of 2020 and 2021 changed the way we all lived our lives, dwarfing all those other problems fans had been grumbling about. Matches at the top few levels of football's pyramid were played, but only behind closed doors. Beyond that, non-league and junior football juddered to a complete halt. Where leagues managed to carry on, the games were played in soulless empty grounds, devoid of all atmosphere – the whole point of our stadiums the way they are is that they were designed to be packed with people.

Mass vaccinations seemed to be allowing us to claw ourselves gradually out of the coronavirus crisis more than a year after it first struck. And then football – and its fans – suffered another hammer blow. This time it was the hugely controversial decision made by six of England's strongest clubs to join a brand new European Super League.

It was revealed in April 2021 that Manchester City, Manchester United, Liverpool, Tottenham Hotspur, Chelsea and Arsenal were going to take part, along with Spanish clubs Real Madrid, Barcelona and Atlético Madrid and the Italian big three of AC Milan, Juventus and Inter. Real Madrid president Florentino Pérez had been elected as the first ESL chairman and he told Spanish TV that the league would be saving football at a critical moment. He explained that action was needed because 'young people are no longer interested in football'.

Condemnation of the plans was universal. And the fact that the proposed new league would be a closed shop with no promotion into it and no relegation from it was the worst blow of all. Football authorities, politicians, royalty, clubs, managers and players all added a unanimously strong voice to the protests. And so too did the fans, who played a huge part in getting the decision overturned within little more than 48 hours. Protecting the loyal supporters was focussed on and spoken about time and time again by everyone who played a part in forcing clubs into the speedy rethink.

Leading the way was former England and Manchester United player Gary Neville, now a top media pundit, who weighed in against the plans with all guns blazing on behalf of fans. 'I'm absolutely disgusted, the plans are a disgrace,' he said on Sky Sports immediately after the ESL was announced. 'There are 100-and-odd years of history in this country from fans who have loved these clubs. Being a big club is not just about having a global fanbase – it's acting properly at the right time. I'm not for everything standing still, but the fans need protecting.'

Neville himself is part-owner of a professional football club so was speaking with particular authority on the matter. So too, of course, is his old team-mate David Beckham. He commented on Instagram, 'I loved football from when I was a young child, and I'm still a fan. As a player and now as an owner, I know that our sport is nothing without the fans. We need football to be for everyone.'

Those two were by no means the only former top players to condemn the plans. Ex-Arsenal striker Ian Wright was furious with his beloved old club for getting involved. 'Is this how far we have fallen?' he asked in a video on Twitter. 'That we are getting into competitions because we are not good enough to get into, so to the detriment of the English game we are getting a seat at the table we have no right to be at.' *Match of the Day* presenter Gary Lineker said, 'If fans stand as one against this anti-football pyramid scheme, it can be stopped in its tracks. We've seen clearly over the last 12 months that football is nothing without fans.' Lineker's colleague Alan Shearer added, 'Where are these owners? Why don't they come out and face the media? Tell us why they've done it, why they want a closed shop that no one else can get in to. These clubs can dress it up how they want, that it's about protecting their interests to protect the wider game – but it's simply about greed.' Former England striker Peter Crouch said, 'It's a disgrace. It shows no regard for the history of our competitions and what those competitions have helped those clubs achieve. We don't need a European Super League – the Premier League has more than enough money and exposure.'

Understandably, the 14 Premier League clubs who would have been left behind were also totally as one in their opposition. Everton led the way with a passionate and damning statement: 'Everton is saddened and disappointed to see proposals of a breakaway league pushed forward by six clubs. Six clubs acting entirely in their own interests. Six clubs tarnishing the reputation of our league and the game. Six clubs choosing to disrespect every other club within the league as well as betraying the majority of football supporters across our country and beyond.

At this time of national and international crisis – and a defining period for our game – clubs should be working together collaboratively with the ideals of our game and its supporters uppermost. This preposterous arrogance is not wanted anywhere in football outside of the clubs that have drafted this plan.'

Everton said it all, really, but other clubs were keen to voice their fierce disapproval. Brighton & Hove Albion said, 'Plans for a European Super League totally disregard fans, the lifeblood of our sport at professional levels, and fly in the face of the views and wishes of the overwhelming majority of football supporters of all clubs.' Leicester City spoke out: 'Football clubs exist for their supporters, whose passion and devotion are not simply a response to the game, but a fundamental and indispensable part of it. Their contribution is fed by their right to dream – a right we share a collective responsibility to protect.' Aston Villa echoed the thoughts of other clubs: 'We are not standing idly by allowing the dreams of Aston Villa fans to be taken away by this sinister scheme.' West Ham's statement read, 'These proposals are an attack on sporting integrity, undermine competition, and ignore those supporters, and those of the thousands of clubs and millions of players, from the Premier League to Sunday League, who can aspire to reach the top of the game. Our supporters have been there throughout our 125-year journey, for our FA Cup and European Cup Winners' Cup wins, our promotions and many other memorable moments.' Wolverhampton Wanderers accused the owners of the six clubs of having 'plotted and schemed to find a way to exist in a small and comfortable bubble' and West Bromwich Albion said they wholly opposed the 'selfish and divisive plans' that no genuine football fan could support. A meeting of the 14 clubs 'unanimously and vigorously rejected' the plans for the Super League and it was announced that they would be considering all possible actions to prevent it from progressing.

Players also added their thoughts, and it was particularly relevant when those who spoke out were with clubs who were part of the proposed breakaway. Liverpool's squad jointly put a message to their owners on social media: 'We don't like it and we don't want it to happen. This is our collective position. Our commitment to this football club and its supporters is absolute and unconditional.' Manchester United and England defender Luke Shaw commented, 'I worry that these proposed changes could impact the sport that I and millions love. We have been without supporters in stadiums for over a year now and I know how much myself and the team have missed them in each and every game. Fans and players should always have a voice and their opinion should always be counted.'

Burnley captain Ben Mee added, 'Footballers play for the fans, not people in boardrooms. No one scores a goal or makes a last-ditch tackle to earn the praise of the owners. They do it for the feeling they get when the crowd roars.' And Leeds United striker Patrick Bamford told Sky Sports, 'I haven't seen one football fan who's happy about it. Football's for the fans – it's important we stand our ground. It's amazing the amount of uproar that comes into the game when someone's pocket is being hurt. It's a shame it's not like this with everything that's going wrong in the game, like racism.'

Bamford was speaking after Leeds (outside the six) had drawn with Liverpool (inside the six) at Elland Road. Supporters were joined by fans from other clubs outside the ground to stage a protest – during which a Liverpool shirt was burned, and a plane flew over the stadium displaying an anti-ESL message. Leeds players warmed up in T-shirts saying 'Earn It' next to the Champions League logo and 'Football is for the fans', and left a spare set of shirts in Liverpool's dressing room in case they wanted to join the protest. That angered Liverpool manager Jürgen Klopp, who pointed out, 'We were not involved in the process. We are the team, we wear the club shirts with pride. Somebody has made a decision with the owners in world football that we don't know exactly why.'

Managers like Klopp were put in the invidious position of being asked about something they personally didn't agree with, but the people paying their wages had signed up to. Manchester City boss Pep Guardiola trod the same dividing line but spoke out about the closed shop issue: 'It is not sport when the relation between effort and success and reward doesn't exist. It is not sport if it doesn't matter if you lose.'

Even royalty got involved in what was a huge media story and the Duke of Cambridge offered, 'More than ever, we must protect the entire football community – from the top level to the grassroots – and the values of competition and fairness at its core. I share the concerns of fans about the proposed Super League and the damage it risks causing to the game we love.'

And, of course, fans are never far from a social media platform. One of the many thousands who tweeted, Manny commented, 'Why don't we fans just unite and say we will not watch the Super League. No eyeballs, no ads, no revenue. Hit them where it hurts – their bottom line. Too naive?' Kevin tweeted that he hoped the six would actually leave the Premier League: 'This would allow the rest of the league to have a more competitive setup. Every club believing they could win the Premier League. At the moment, it's only the dreams of a handful, and they want out.' And Andy warned, 'Who in this day and age can afford to buy a football club? Anyone that does it doesn't do it for the love of the game, they do it as an investment to make money from. Get the blinkers off, football fans, this is the reality.'

While the professionals who earn their living from the game were sticking up for the fans, the supporters themselves were taking direct action. About 1,000 Chelsea followers had gathered outside Stamford Bridge while the team were preparing to play a midweek Premier League game against Brighton. Top effort, that, as they'd far rather have been allowed inside to watch the match than stand outside parading their banners and voicing their angry thoughts. It was while the protest was going on that word filtered out about Chelsea and Manchester City having second thoughts over the whole plan. Within hours, it had collapsed like a house of cards as the other four English clubs followed suit. Max tweeted, 'Say what you want about the ESL, the knock-out stages are exciting …' Mark added, 'I'll tell you one thing this European Super League bollocks has done. Brought 99.9 per cent of football fans who are usually at each other's throats together in shared disgust.' England and Manchester City star Raheem Sterling also took to Twitter to succinctly sum it all up in two words: 'Ok, bye.'

UEFA president Aleksander Čeferin said the six English clubs were 'back in the fold', adding, 'The important thing now is that we move on, rebuild the unity that the game enjoyed before this and move forward together.'

Leeds had played a prominent part in fighting the ESL plans. Chief executive Angus Kinnear wrote in the matchday programme for a game with Manchester United days after the plans were ditched: 'They were a betrayal of every true football supporter. It was a disgrace that managers and players were left to defend the indefensible while owners cowered at home.'

ESL chairman Florentino Pérez reflected, 'Maybe we didn't explain it well, but they also didn't give us an opportunity to explain it. I've never seen threats like this. It was like we killed someone. It was like we killed football. But we were trying to work out how to save football.'

Owners of the six English clubs offered apologies for getting involved in the first place and Liverpool chief executive Billy Hogan promised to do all he could to win back the supporters' trust. Chelsea said the club had feared damage to its reputation and alienating fans, as well as undermining some of its campaigning and community work. They said that the original decision to sign up was because they didn't want to fall behind some of their closest rivals. The European Super League was no more, but bet your life the idea will resurface another fine day when no one's looking.

Despite the U-turn, fans continued to take to the streets outside stadiums, now directing their anger elsewhere. Arsenal supporters staged a dramatic mass protest where club owner Stan Kroenke was the subject of a brilliant pun on one of the banners: 'Pin the fail on the Kroenke'. A lot of thought had gone into another banner: 'You stole our crest, we stayed/You took our home, we moved/Wherever you went, we followed/Whatever price you want, we paid/All for you to go and sell our soul!' At Manchester United, supporters revived a colourful protest of ten years previously which they staged against the club owners by focussing on the green-and-gold colours of Newton Heath, the club's original name back in the 19th century. And then they stepped it up a notch with a protest that was so strong and well supported that it prevented a match with Liverpool taking place at Old Trafford. Although the more outrageous aspects of their protest were widely condemned, the ensuing publicity was enormous and would undoubtedly have been heard loud and clear in the US homes of the owners.

The whole angry, bitter, divisive and ultimately pathetic ESL debacle certainly helped secure the place of the football fan at the heart of the game. And perhaps this new-found fan power could be put to future good use. Having a say on how VAR is used? Helping stamp out the scourge of racism? Getting a place in a club's boardroom? In Germany, at least 51 per cent of a club must be owned by fans and, of course, Bayern Munich – along with Paris Saint-Germain – were significantly absent from the 12 clubs originally involved in the ESL. This whole improbable saga could prove an important stepping stone towards a bigger involvement in the game for fans.

2

Que sera, sera, whatever will be will be

THERE WAS a sign behind the goal at Manchester United during the 2020/21 lockdowns caused by the coronavirus pandemic which said, 'Football is nothing without fans'. It was there to acknowledge that matches were being played in the weirdest of atmospheres at the time with fans banned from attending to prevent the further spread of the virus. The Stretford End quote – big enough to get hit more than once by off-target shots – was attributed to legendary former United manager Sir Matt Busby.

All very good, and lovely for the fans to feel valued as they sat at home on their sofas watching the matches on TV. And, of course, supporters were missed dreadfully by the clubs and the players – their noise, their banter, their wit, the atmosphere they create, their lack of respect for the opposition.

All of us just couldn't wait to get back into grounds again to greet our mates, perform our little rituals, support our team, abuse the VAR system, get silly when a goal's scored.

Yet, it's not quite true, is it? That football is nothing without fans. Better, for sure, but not nothing. I used to regularly slip through a broken-down bit of fencing round a recreation ground to stop and watch a local league game for ten or so minutes on my way to the main match I was going to see on a Saturday afternoon. I would boost the attendance by about 50 per cent as the match was played out in front of one cold-looking girlfriend and a man with a dog. But the players didn't care whether there were fans watching or not, this was the game they'd looked forward to all week. The one who was a bit too good for this level but knew it and dribbled too much. The one who used to be a bit of a player but was now too old and still refusing to retire. The one who'd clearly been drafted in to make up the numbers and looked as bored by it all as the dog with the other spectator. And the referee, trying to control the whole match without setting foot out of the centre circle. Football is every bit as important to the players at this level as it is to the superstars at Old Trafford. Well, perhaps not quite as vital, but still something to get passionate and excited about and dissect in great detail down the pub afterwards.

Incidentally, Celtic fans were far from impressed at Sir Matt Busby being credited for the 'Football is nothing without fans' quote. They immediately claimed it was something said by their own legend of a former manager, Jock Stein. It had been put up by United after the club asked fans which message they'd choose to see at the Stretford

End. One of them, Rick, tweeted, 'We suggested they sent a heartfelt message to show just how much the club, players and manager value their match-going supporters.'

So why did these 'much-valued' supporters become fans in the first place? Liking, even loving, watching football was a prerequisite. But when they were prevented from going to the ground by lockdowns, and only able to watch matches that were televised, many admitted they missed even more the other things that went with it. Meeting for a pint beforehand, singing along in the ground with their mates, enjoying the company of like-minded people. It was the group ethic they missed most, the feeling of belonging to a band of brothers (and sisters!) who loved doing the same things and yearned for the same result.

From an early age we started to learn the lessons that being a football fan teaches. Loyalty, commitment, enthusiasm, belonging. Even a feeling that if you shout loud enough, and put as much passion into your support as the players do into the game, then you, too, can make a difference. Along the way, you pick up the habits and traditions of being a committed fan. Taking the same route to the ground every time, stopping for refreshments at the same place, even wearing the same lucky pants. Though we won't go into those too much.

And hopefully never get as superstitious about such things as former Chelsea coach Maurizio Sarri. It's said he once crashed his car into one of his team's BMW in the car park before a match when he was managing in one of Italy's lower leagues. The team won, so the following home match the players watched in astonishment as Sarri recreated the crash with the same BMW in the same car park as he assumed it would bring good luck again. Well, good luck for him, maybe not so much for the poor battered Beamer.

There's also a tradition carried out by Mark Taylor's friend to decide who's going to win that afternoon. Writing in *The Sportsman*, Mark said, 'He would throw his chewing gum towards a specific grid near Bolton Wanderers' stadium before every home game, and its landing place would determine how the team would do that afternoon. Straight in the grid, home win. Hopeless miss, away win. Land on a grid bar, draw. It's this kind of nonsensical ritual which makes football fans such a rare breed.' I wonder if he ever took it so seriously that if his spitting bit of gum missed completely he'd turn round and go home again, as there then would be no point going on to endure the disappointment of the match.

Once inside the ground, the fans unite in optimism about what the day will bring, mixed with apprehension about how they'll feel if it all goes wrong. There's still more tasks to be carried out, singing the right songs and the relevant chants at the appropriate moments, backing the team at all times, taunting the opposition and their fans whenever possible. The fans see themselves as the team's 12th man – there to motivate their own side, as well as their additional role of intimidating the other lot. And, of course, they've got to be there to celebrate the goals when – if – they come along. There's a lot of work to do for the committed fan.

Unless there's a midweek game, the feelgood factor from a successful Saturday lasts until Wednesday. From then it's all about the anticipation, the gradually building excitement, the chance to do it all again the following weekend. Only better.

And then there's the away days. Now they really are the highlight of a fan's week. The journey there, travel plans devised by the supporter who's an expert at that sort of thing, and the whistle-whetting pub stops that are a key part of a grand day out. Everything is heightened in terms of passion and excitement when you're far from home. An away goal is celebrated wildly, an away win even more so. 'Oh what fun it is to see (your team) win away.' I'm sure he was just being amusing but after possibly one too many televised matches because of lockdown (we'll come to more about that in a minute), Garry Davies tweeted, 'I've realised I'm not a football fan at all. I'm actually a fan of cans on the train and being in a pub at 10am. The actual football is boring.' Or, as Elis James lamented during the enforced time-out, 'All I'm asking for is an away trip, a late winner (3-2, having been second best all afternoon), the players to punch the air in front of us at full time and for a man whose name I don't know but have been on nodding terms with since 2001 to compliment my new coat.'

Of course, away trips so often end in disappointment and supporters are well used to that. It comes with the territory. I remember talking to a Football League manager who told me what it was like in his house the day after his team had lost. He would be moody, short with his children, sharp-tongued to his wife, unable to shake off the all-consuming gloom that defeat had imposed on him. 'When my kids wished me goodnight at their bedtime I felt ashamed and horrified at how little I'd given them all day, and how my mood had depressed the whole house. I always vow I'll handle it differently the next time but, of course, I don't.'

That may have been the manager's experience, constantly rewinding whether it was his fault for picking the wrong team and tactics, or his players for not carrying out his instructions properly, or the referee for getting all the big decisions wrong. But the diehard fan feels it too, a day ruined by 11 players losing a football match they could/should have won. Well, not ruined, just spoiled a little bit. There's still been a lot of laughs on the way there and back, some tasty food and thirst-quenching drinks downed. A day spent with good friends sharing the same excitement and fanaticism can hardly have been wasted. As the lead character in the Ken Loach film *Looking for Eric* says of the power of football, 'It just fills you up so much that you forget all the shit in your life, even just for a few hours.'

Hopefully there's no sort of unspoken assumption in all that's been said so far that the fan being described has to be a man. Nothing could be further from the truth. It's not a prerequisite of being a football follower, and girls and women are certainly a part of every army of supporters. Once upon a time, well in the 19th century to be exact, women were allowed into some football grounds for free as it was thought it would improve the behaviour of the men. But the experiment was abandoned as free entry for women became so popular that it was costing clubs too much money.

So whoever you are or whatever your background, it's pretty much an all-consuming commitment once you become a passionate and loyal football fan. What it felt like was defined by Newcastle supporter Andy Smart in a *Guardian* interview in 2005: 'An idiot? Me? I'm a Newcastle fan, for God's sake – I'm not an idiot! I live in Lancashire and complete a 300-mile round trip for every home game. I haven't missed one since 1992. I follow Newcastle around the country and in Europe. I'm not an idiot, I'm effing deluded!' Another fan, Chris, joining in an online discussion about why people followed football, summed it up: 'We're fucking saddoes, that's all there is to it!'

What with all that passion – and delusion – devoted fans suffer such intense levels of stress while watching a match that they're at risk of a heart attack. We sort of assumed that anyway but researchers at Oxford University have done all the tests to prove it. They found levels of the hormone cortisol soared in the saliva of Brazil supporters watching their team's shock 7-1 hammering by Germany in the 2014 World Cup semi-final. Cortisol increases blood pressure and so puts an added burden on the heart. Researcher Dr Martha Newson told the BBC that many fans were sobbing, but others used coping mechanisms such as humour and hugging to reduce the stress. She thought lights should be dimmed at grounds at the end of matches, and soothing music played over the PA to help losing fans cope with a defeat. We're still waiting for that – and guess what, it's never going to happen!

It wasn't heart attacks or the lack of soothing music that brought football to a dramatic and unexpected halt in 2020. It was a worldwide virus that caused every one of us to re-evaluate what we liked about life itself. And, very soon after that, what we liked about being a football fan and how much we were about to miss it.

3

Empty grounds: It's all gone quiet over there

THE CORONAVIRUS pandemic of 2020 and 2021 swept remorselessly through all our lives, killing beyond 125,000 people in the UK, many of them devoted football supporters.

The last match I saw before all football stopped due to the first wave of the pandemic was Fulham against Preston in the Championship. That was on 29 February 2020. I remember being in a mood somewhere between apprehension and complacency – we realised something bad and way out of our control was about to happen. But surely, we reassured ourselves, we'd be careful and make sure we remained untouched by it all. Storm clouds may have been gathering, and when well over 100,000 people died of the virus here and millions more around the world, the analogy with the Second World War became a legitimate one. We all just milled about Craven Cottage before the game as if nothing more than a home win was on our minds. Any late arrival had to shuffle cheek by jowl along the line of fans to reach their seats, the same as always and as close to each other as always. Social distancing and face masks weren't part of our vocabulary at the time.

Fulham won 2-0 and it turned out to be the last game to take place at the ground in front of fans for more than a year. After the match, my son Will and I walked back through the park by the Thames and then watched as my eldest brother climbed the stairs to Putney Bridge underground station along with hundreds of others. All three of us, I think, thought we'd soon be putting this temporary nuisance of a virus panic firmly behind us.

Football drifted on for a couple more weeks, shutting down after a last hurrah (or olé, as it turned out) at Anfield where Liverpool played Atlético Madrid in the Champions League on 11 March. There was a lot of talk that the match should never have been played – for footballing reasons alone Liverpool probably agreed as they lost and got knocked out of the tournament. Coronavirus had already forced a lockdown in Spain, with Madrid the worst affected city, yet thousands of their fans were allowed to travel to the UK and were packed in among a crowd of 52,267.

Writing in *The Independent*, Liverpool fan Neil Atkinson said afterwards, 'I think one of the things the whole fandango before and after the Atlético game shows is a lack of awareness, interest and care from decision makers in Government on what attending football matches – especially European ones – actually entails. Those of us who go to games know that it tends to be an enterprise. You do not magically appear in your seat and then magically disappear afterwards. Ministers and dignitaries may be whisked in and out of sporting events. You and I are not. You board public transport and planes, you eat and drink and share spaces, you congregate in pubs and on concourses. You go out after. We went out after. Went out because we knew it was the last time.'

Of course, the evening came to an end and everyone went home eventually, but the damage had been done. Infections were definitely spread that night and football was again a target for criticism by publicity-hungry politicians. We soon went into a full lockdown – Joe Wicks, banana bread and TikTok.

Off the pitch, the financial effects were devastating and many non-playing staff soon lost their jobs. Premier League clubs were able to continue to get considerable income from TV rights as soon as matches resumed, but lower down the football pyramid there wasn't that lifeline. Times were hard.

Suspending the Premier League on 9 March 2020 was unavoidable but not everyone saw eye to eye on what should happen next. West Ham vice-chair Karren Brady said the season should be declared null and void but others pointed out that it would be unjust if runaway leaders Liverpool were denied the title.

Social media was predictably full of opinions, with someone going by the name of G messaging, 'Really don't see why they can't play behind closed doors. Lots of people more vulnerable than them carrying on with their life. We could all do with some entertainment and a sense of normality. In wartime singers and comedians would fly out to war zones to entertain the troops.'

Days turned into weeks and it was three months before those Premier League entertainers were allowed back to perform for us and finish their 2019/20 season. Lockdown was strange and tough for everybody and just because you were a famous footballer you weren't immune from struggling to cope with it. Manchester City and England defender Kyle Walker told Henry Winter in an interview in *The Times*, 'I had dark moments. I was sat in my flat thinking what's my life come to? When we were allowed back to football that was my release, not think about anything, just do the thing I love.'

When it did finally return, Premier League matches could only be seen on television as no fans were allowed in the grounds. It was all so eerie and unsatisfactory. Some clubs filled seats with cardboard cut-outs, crowd noise (with the emphasis on noise!) was played over the PA, teams walked out separately, players didn't shake hands, substitutes sat socially distanced from each other, coaching staff wore masks, players' screams when fouled, as well as their swear words, were all too audible, as were managers' comments from the sidelines. In addition, touching each other when celebrating a goal wasn't supposed to happen but players couldn't resist a cuddle and a huddle in the excitement. When it became the subject for a bit of national uproar later in the pandemic, a few players – Harry Kane and James Maddison among them – looked as if they'd got the memo, but others carried on celebrating regardless. Which was all fair enough, probably, as players were getting tested very regularly to make sure they didn't have the virus, and anyway they weren't the ones in the greatest jeopardy from Covid-19. It would have been the poor old fans, especially elderly ones, more at risk of serious illness or even death. Which is why the stadiums looked so forlorn and sad without people in them.

For the great majority of the time that they were told to stay indoors and keep away from football, the fans were totally obedient. It broke down a bit, though, when Liverpool clinched the Premier League title in July. The trophy was presented inside the ground but thousands couldn't resist going out on the night of all nights to celebrate the club's overdue success. Assistant Chief Constable Natalie Perischine, of Merseyside Police, had pointed out the danger of further lockdown measures in the city if there was a spike in cases caused by people mixing on the streets. She said, 'The club and TV companies have made careful preparations to ensure that millions of people can enjoy these special moments on screen, in the comfort of their homes. On this occasion, the best seat in the house is in your living room.' The same problem recurred when Glasgow Rangers won the Scottish Premiership the following season and thousands just couldn't resist breaking lockdown to hold a celebration party outside the ground.

The virus had a bit of a lie-down in the summer and a new 2020/21 season started on schedule for non-elite clubs with fans allowed in as long as they took sensible safeguards. Temperature checks, social distancing, hand sanitisers, no touching the ball, no shaking of hands. The Premier League resumed in September, having had just a

FOOTBALL IS BETTER WITH FANS

short break since the much-delayed end to the previous season. But by the end of October much of non-league was suspended again as coronavirus cases began to rise. However, there was light at the end of the tunnel for the Premier League when it was announced that some fans would be allowed to return to stadiums – well, some of the stadiums, anyway – at the end of that November.

During the crazy fan-free months, good on any manager who never forgot that just because supporters were out of sight they weren't out of mind. Arsenal's Mikel Arteta said during a painful run of results that coincided with the virus and stadiums being empty, 'We need to win football matches and when we don't, I feel like I am letting the club down and the people that work for us, and obviously our fans.' After a big win in an empty ground for the successful Chelsea women's team she manages, Emma Hayes put it nicely when she tweeted, 'To our fans, we heard you the whole time.' Manchester United boss Ole Gunnar Solskjaer had only one regret after his team thrashed Leeds 6-2 during that time: 'It's just unfortunate we can't celebrate it with our fans.' And later in the season he admitted using the return of fans as a bargaining tool in negotiations to keep striker Edinson Cavani at the club for another season. Solskjaer said, 'I want him to experience Old Trafford full and scoring at the Stretford End. There's no better feeling.'

Well, Old Trafford wasn't exactly full, but Cavani found out for himself soon after just what it was like to score in front of the fans there. He struck a spectacular goal from 40 yards against Fulham in May 2021 when home supporters – well, 10,000 of them – were allowed back in to the ground for the first time in more than a year.

Social media inevitably weighed in with more opinions. Someone calling themselves Snape said, 'Football is not that important right now but long term, football and sport will be a great way to get over this. Let's hope so anyway and not too many lose their lives.' Humphrey the Helicopter flew in: 'Jürgen Klopp said it all. Even one life is more important than football. We all have far more pressing things to be getting on with.' Brass Eye continued, 'Better get the Subbuteo down from the loft and dust it off then.' Saint J commented, 'I love my football as much as the next person but it really just pales into insignificance now with what's going on. Stay safe everyone, whoever you support.' Sean said, 'I'm a pathetic grown man and parent whose mood and lockdown mental wellbeing can often be dictated by how my football team gets on. Happy days. Let's all have a bevvy.'

Burnley striker Jay Rodriguez was refreshingly quick to show where his priorities were. He tweeted, 'Fans weren't in the stands when the new season started but we still had to please them.' And he showed his compassion later with another message to supporters: 'Nobody should feel alone during what is a difficult time. If any Burnley fans are feeling low or you know anybody who needs support, my DMs are open. Drop me a message with as many details as possible and I'll help in any way I can. Let's all look after each other.' Good for Jay, but perhaps he could have a word with 'Pathetic' Sean who complained that his mental wellbeing is dictated by how his team gets on!

Some clubs were able to allow a limited number of supporters in to watch matches on TV screens in the hospitality areas of their grounds – as long as they didn't have a direct view of the pitch. Millwall said such schemes were 'imperative from a financial point of view for clubs who had been left to fend for themselves throughout this crisis'. Cinemas were also permitted to show some live games to socially distanced fans but West Ham manager David Moyes wasn't the only one to wonder out loud why it was safer to be in an indoor cinema than at an outdoor football ground. Manchester United executive vice-chairman Ed Woodward questioned why football fans should be treated differently to those attending indoor concerts, and Football Supporters' Association chairman Malcolm Clarke told the BBC that fans being able to watch matches in hospitality lounges but not in the stands showed the rules to be illogical. There was also much sympathy for lower-league clubs when they drew top-level opposition at home in the FA Cup and fans – particularly youngsters – were deprived of possibly a once-in-a-lifetime opportunity to see the visiting superstars. After his team lost bravely to Manchester City in the 2020/21 fourth round, Cheltenham Town manager Michael Duff said, 'The one crying shame is that for the biggest game in the club's 134-year history the supporters weren't there.'

The effects of lockdown and playing in front of an empty stadium were on the mind of Phil McNulty, the BBC's chief football writer, when he reported on Spurs' third successive defeat (1-0 at home to Chelsea in February 2021). He wrote, 'While no manager would ever say they would welcome the absence of supporters in these times of behind-closed-doors games, it would have been very interesting to hear how this tactical approach would have been received had it been carried out in the presence of 60,000 fans. The smart money would have been on mutiny. It is hard to imagine Tottenham supporters, had they been here, standing for this negative approach in patient silence. In fact, they probably would not have stood for it at all.' It was often felt that it was better for a struggling team to actually be playing in empty grounds rather than in front of frustrated and agitated – though still passionate – supporters. Any unease off the pitch might have further undermined morale and confidence on it.

It's pretty clear that pandemic lockdowns proved that football is better with fans. There's the atmosphere created, the build-up, the anticipation, the sense of belonging, the pleasure it brings, the joy of winning. And that's just for the supporters. Managers missed us too, players missed us, the club's accountants missed us (!). We had to patiently get used to going without, and of course it was never going to be forever. Despite Liverpool legend Bill Shankly's famous quote about football being more important than life and death, we knew during that weird time it wasn't. Staying alive and avoiding the virus took precedence over sport.

But did playing without fans make any actual difference on the pitch? It was still 11 v 11 under the guidance of a referee you weren't ever going to agree with. And, at Premier League level, with a VAR system that was even harder and more controversial to deal with. Tactics didn't change, formations didn't change, the pitch was the same shape and colour and so were the rules. That only really leaves mental attitude – was the challenge of playing at a stadium like Anfield or Old Trafford, say, any easier for away teams when the stands were forlornly vacant and the shouts of players and managers weren't drowned out by the fans? Did the home team miss out on drawing inspiration and energy from their crowd?

Yes, no doubt about it. Clubs did better in away games than previously, and, for instance, the home form of champions Liverpool slumped when the lockdown slammed all doors shut again in December 2020. From being unbeaten at home for three years, a total of 68 games, they lost an incredible six times in a row – to Burnley, Brighton, Manchester City, Everton, Chelsea and Fulham. They didn't manage a goal from open play in any of those matches and it was their worst sequence of results ever at Anfield.

There were contributory reasons, or some people not so sympathetic might call them excuses. Confidence and belief slips away once you lose a few and it's hard for any team, even champions, to suddenly snap out of a poor run. And they'd suffered badly from injuries in a season over-packed with game after game to make up for lost time. Outstanding central defender Virgil van Dijk was one of those missed the most and I loved a tweet on the subject by Amy O'Connor: 'I just mindlessly asked my boyfriend if he missed Van Dijk and he solemnly replied "I think about him every day".'

The impact of playing in an empty stadium wasn't lost on either manager before Liverpool and Manchester City met in February 2021 at Anfield. Press conferences the day before a match have to be taken with a pinch of salt as managers often use the occasion to say what they think the opposition don't want to hear, playing mind games and ruffling a few feathers. On this occasion, Liverpool's Jürgen Klopp was adamant that not having fans present would be crucial. He said, 'We all know how much they help. We have to make sure the atmosphere without them doesn't make a difference on the field.' And Pep Guardiola commented at City's media briefing, 'There's something about Anfield that you will find in no other stadium in the world. You feel small and that the rival players are all over you. It's a bugger of a ground.' After City won the match by a distance, 4-1, Guardiola returned to the point, 'Anfield is so intimidating and for many years we were not able to win here. Hopefully next time we can do it with people.'

Now a top pundit, Jamie Carragher played more than 700 games for Liverpool so when he talked in his 2020 book, *The Greatest Games*, about playing at Anfield, you couldn't find a more expert witness. He wrote, 'Is it the greatest atmosphere in world football? I could not impartially declare that. I am sure there are stadiums across Europe and South America where supporters are as noisy or intimidating. But they cannot be more influential. I always felt we had an immediate and obvious advantage as Anfield is quite small. Although it's been regularly upgraded, its compactness has never been compromised. The layout lends itself to a cage fight with supporters so close to the action they can stare into the players' eyes. I loved hearing former Arsenal manager Arsène Wenger saying it's the hardest place to play in Europe. "It's the only place where you can take a corner and shake hands with supporters"!'

One fan analysed the challenge for Liverpool of playing at an empty ground. Amar Singh tweeted, 'Talk of Anfield not being a fortress any more is nonsensical. Without fans it's just a patch of grass with four empty stands. Nobody dreads playing in an empty stadium.'

The gloom about playing empty stadiums was felt everywhere and Barcelona genius Lionel Messi told it like it was. 'It's horrible to play without fans, it's a very ugly sensation,' he said in an interview with Spanish newspaper *Marca*. 'Seeing no one in the stadium is like a training session and it is very tough to really get going at the start of a game. The pandemic has caused football to change a lot, and for the worse. You can see it in the matches, and I hope this all ends soon and we can get fans back into the stadiums and return to normality.'

The view was international. Chelsea's Mason Mount said before an England game, 'We miss the fans. We want them back. We just want to go out and put on a good show for them. We want to lift their spirits and make them happy.'

Wolves player Rúben Neves told the *Daily Mail*, 'It's impossible to be the same as when fans are there. The adrenaline, the intensity. We can hear everything being said, the sound of the ball when we pass it. It's really hard to keep the same focus. I hope football will be the same as before when fans come back. To play with a full stadium again will be amazing.'

Playing a top-level match in an empty stadium means a team are less 'aroused'. That was the result of an investigation by England rugby manager Eddie Jones to explain why the national team seemed to lack their normal level of aggression in matches played during the lockdowns with no fans present. He said a study in Austria reaching those conclusions had been carried out into football matches played by Salzburg. It found there had been fewer 'emotional situations' and Jones concluded, 'Without fans present, games are tending to be less aggressive generally in rugby, and it has been the same in football.'

Incidentally, I've often thought football could learn more lessons from studying other sports. I was watching a hockey match many years ago and the coach was yelling instructions at his forwards about when they should be pressing. One player wasn't allowed to do it alone as the opposition could easily bypass him, it had to be two or three pressing simultaneously for the 'strangle' to work. It was the sort of tactic that became commonplace in football years later but was something I'd never considered before.

The pandemic took a new and even stronger grip in the winter months of the 2020/21 season. Football at most levels outside the very highest was halted and fans everywhere remained sidelined. It seemed a bit pathetic to moan that we all missed going to a match, but miss it we did. It was a horrible time and took us up to and beyond the first anniversary of when it all began to fall apart.

4

Fans return: What's it like to see a crowd?

HAVING BEEN kept away from almost all professional football for eight months, fans were finally permitted into Premier League stadiums at the beginning of December 2020. Only 2,000 at a time, and only at some of the grounds, so it was still a matter of luck as to who actually got the golden tickets. Just like at the non-league games mentioned in the last chapter, there were all sorts of protocols put on supporters – temperature checks, face masks at all times, socially distant seating. Supporters were told not to touch the ball if it came near them, not to hug or touch each other, and not to approach players for autographs or pictures. But they were allowed to sing. Even if badly in most cases.

Leeds manager Marcelo Bielsa objected to the return of fans in just some of the grounds. Yorkshire, along with Manchester, was still in the Government's top tier of virus restrictions, so no supporters were permitted at Elland

Road. 'They should not be allowed in at all elsewhere until everybody is allowed,' said Bielsa. 'It should be about trying to maintain the competition as equal as possible as the presence of fans has an effect on the results.'

Away fans weren't permitted at all but a few enterprising Sheffield Wednesday supporters got round that on the first weekend back in the Championship by booking pitch-facing rooms in a Holiday Inn that overlooks Norwich's ground. They flew banners out of the windows and even occasionally outsang the 2,000 home supporters who'd actually paid to be inside the ground.

Elsewhere, it was nothing but pleasure and relief to be back at a match on a Saturday afternoon. 'I've been stuck at home shielding so this is a godsend to me,' said one fan. 'It's like winning the lottery to get a ticket,' said a Spurs supporter before the north London derby, 'and for it to be against Arsenal of all teams is just such a bonus.' And Darren on Twitter commented, 'Parking the car, moaning in the restaurant, walking in the rain, hearing the programme sellers, going through the tunnel, up the stairs and we are there. Even standing in the rain was worth it.'

Arsenal fan Sam Blitz told the *Daily Mail*, 'From the moment the first chant was sung – a customary "What do you think of Tottenham" 15 minutes before kick-off – 272 days of waiting came to an end. It showed that going to football matches is much more than the 90 minutes. It's about the community you go with, the familiar faces you see in the stands, the banter with the away fans. And it was a bonus that the post-match queues for the tube were much shorter.'

Tim Stillman, who describes himself as a bedroom blogger and professional Arsenal fan, said, 'Never did I foresee attending an Arsenal game with muffled singing beneath mandatory face masks. I was at the final match at Highbury and the first game at the Emirates but in years to come how will I view attending the first game with fans allowed back at Emirates Stadium during a pandemic? It's not possible to meet a group of mates and a handful of acquaintances in the pub. Instead, 12 of us gathered in two groups of six underneath a railway bridge and drank from tins like 14-year olds. I didn't expect to become emotional but as we entered through the turnstiles and the stewards applauded the fans one by one it choked me up. Though this was not a return to normality by any means, it was a night for reconnection – with the players, our friends, our matchday muscle memory. It was a reminder that to be a fan is to be part of a community and that a matchday is a precious ritual.'

Then there was 61-year-old Luton fan Clive Stallwood. 'I'll explain it as a football cliché – I'm over the moon,' he told *The Independent*. 'It's fantastic. I've been going to football for 50 years and every other Saturday. It's been like missing a tooth. I did miss going to the pub before the game but you can't have it all.'

Norwich City supporter David Powles said, 'Each player came out of the tunnel and headed straight to the South Stand to show their appreciation. The fans responded with chants and cheers. Boy, did that feel good. And once the game began it was wonderful just how quickly it all felt normal again. Within 30 seconds no less, a fan slated the defence for failing to pass the ball quickly enough. After nine months I think that bloke really needed to get that out of his system. It mattered a lot to be back doing the thing I love with like-minded people.'

It was seeing old friends again that appealed most to Charlton fan Stavros Demetriades. He told BBC Sport, 'Football is important as a means of socialising and it's also a form of escapism as it helps you focus for a couple of hours on things other than everyday life issues. It felt like home-from-home and, although a little surreal with only 2,000 people in attendance, it was wonderful to be back after so long away.'

The result didn't really matter to Terry Wilby, a Cambridge United fan: 'It felt a bit like a pre-season friendly, in that the result was not important in the greater scheme of things. The fact we were able to watch a game meant we all won, although three points would have been nice as well!'

Jaden Christy, a Leyton Orient supporter, didn't mince his words. 'To me, Orient is everything, my whole life revolves around the club. Saturdays and Tuesdays are only for Orient and nothing else,' he told the *i*. 'Simple things like going to the Coach and Horses with my dad and brother pre-match. It's the little things you miss so much.'

'I am absolutely delighted,' Wycombe fan Jeff Harvey told the PA news agency before his side's Championship game against Stoke. 'It was odd with only a handful of people walking down the road and the weather wasn't great, but we didn't let that spoil anything.'

And of course the love was felt both ways. Never one to hide his emotions, Covid-19 or not, Liverpool manager Jürgen Klopp raved about the return of the limited 2,000 fans to Anfield after the nine-month absence as they beat Wolves 4-0. It was the first time supporters had been allowed in since a few days before the lockdown started, when Liverpool were dumped out of the Champions League by Atlético Madrid.

Klopp said after the Wolves game, 'Wasn't it the perfect night? When we came out, we all had goosebumps. I had no idea how it would feel. It was perfect. The noise, what the people did, they were on their toes, you could see and feel and smell. They had waited so long for it. They started "You'll Never Walk Alone" – really nice. I never knew it could feel that good. We've been waiting to get normality back. Normality is good.' Good old Jürgen summed it up nicely: 'It is so much more enjoyable with people involved.'

Across the city, Everton's Gylfi Sigurdsson got the only goal of the game against Chelsea the first day fans returned after 287 days away. He said, 'It was fantastic, you've almost forgotten what it's like to play in front of fans, it's been that long. You get that buzz. There were only 2,000 in the stadium but it felt like 20,000.' His manager, Carlo Ancelotti, thought it was almost a game-changer: 'The fans made a lot of difference, it was a totally different atmosphere. It made me happy, and I hope the stadium will be full as soon as possible.' Everton CEO Denise Barrett-Baxendale wrote to those who attended the game to thank them for their support, saying, 'The role fans played had a huge impact on our manager and his players. There is no doubt our 12th man helped the players get over the line in securing such a rewarding and deserved victory. Hearing songs from the crowd really was spine-tingling.'

One supporter, Carl Steen, told the *Liverpool Echo* about the occasion: 'You have to do your Covid test, you've got to take your ID, face mask, hand sanitiser – don't touch the rails, don't touch the things you're not supposed to touch. You go and speak to someone to get your ticket scanned, then someone else to get your ID checked, then someone else to get a wristband. It was a bit of a long-winded process but everyone was dead polite and really helpful.'

Another fan, Matt Jones, said, 'At first you're a bit conscious of singing with no one near you but after a while everyone flung themselves into it. I think the players fed off that. The whole matchday experience is something people will never take for granted again, but that particular part is climactic and it was brilliant to experience it again.'

'We have huge respect for the game and prepare as normal, but it's just not been the same,' said Magda Eriksson, captain of the Chelsea women's team, a Sweden international and a columnist for the *i*. She wrote, 'Football as entertainment and, moreover, as a unifying activity that can engage so many people is ultimately reliant on the whole experience in which fans play a massive part. Winning in front of your fans really is a whole different feeling.'

Manchester United experienced the same comparatively small amount of fans allowed in to the West Ham ground in early December. Manager Ole Gunnar Solskjaer said in his programme notes for the club's next match, 'Even though it was just 2,000 fans, it reminded everyone just how good it feels to have that presence in the stands, and we can't wait to open the doors to Old Trafford once again.'

Much-loved Wycombe Wanderers manager Gareth Ainsworth did a lap of the pitch before his team's first game back to return the applause of the club's fans. They responded with a standing ovation. 'It was fantastic,' he told the BBC. 'We won a throw-in in the first minute and they cheered like it was a goal. It was eight months of frustration, desire and need coming out in that moment. It was a joy to see supporters back here with us.'

Mansfield Town manager Nigel Clough told the *Daily Mail*, 'Within ten minutes of the fans being back, a player will give the ball away and it will be "oh you're crap". That would be a time we know we're back to normal. Yes, we miss them. A good football club should always be at the heart of its community.'

It was the same all over Europe, and Honvéd goalkeeper Robi Levkovich contributed his thoughts: 'It's more exciting, more emotional, it's more of a real show than to play without fans. Everyone can see that you play much better with fans. The level of play is better. It pushes you more. You play not just for yourself, you play for them. They shout at you and you give them more.'

Just to bring them all down a peg or two, one anonymous fan had his own Twitter view, which I'm sure he thought was highly amusing. It was on whether or not he wanted to be one of the 2,000 chosen to return for a particular match: 'Hope I don't win the lottery for a ticket! Haven't we suffered enough?' And Duncan Alexander, someone who always has something amusing or insightful to say, thoughtfully tweeted, 'Incredibly nostalgic for the innocent days of no fans at stadiums. The quiet glory. The ball skidding down a relatively banal printed seat cover. The reliability of the artificial crowd noise operator.'

The return of fans, if only in limited numbers, didn't last much longer than what seemed five minutes as the virus made another very strong comeback, and in December 2020 lockdown resumed. It went on until April when it was finally eased for an FA Cup semi-final at Wembley when 4,000 supporters were allowed into the stadium for Leicester v Southampton, provided they could all prove they'd been Covid-tested. Excited Leicester fan Luke told *Sportsmail*, 'It's like the Willy Wonka golden ticket, isn't it?' A week later, that number was doubled as 8,000 virus-tested fans were allowed into Wembley for the Carabao Cup Final when Manchester City beat Spurs 1-0. It was the biggest crowd at a sporting event in the country for more than a year and a further step along the road to recovery from the pandemic. City's Riyad Mahrez said, 'The fans made a massive difference and we look forward to having them back.' His manager, Pep Guardiola, grabbed the chance to thank fans who turned out to line the streets and welcome the team to the Etihad Stadium before their Champions League semi-final a week later. 'We loved it,' he said. 'It was weird playing a semi-final in an empty stadium and our fans should have been there for it. The club belongs to the people.'

The FA Cup final itself was used as a test event for allowing more and more corona-tested fans to watch a game again and 21,000 were allowed in to Wembley. Particularly for fans of the winning Leicester team, it was a memorable afternoon full of passion, enthusiasm, drama, noise, atmosphere and excitement. TV presenter Dan Walker summed it up, 'Aren't fans brilliant? Football – sport – is so much poorer without them.' In the following week, up to 10,000 home fans were allowed back for each of the last couple of Premier League games of the season. Brighton fought back from 2-0 down against already-crowned champions Manchester City to win 3-2 and goalscorer Dan Burn commented, 'I don't think we'd have come back without the fans. It's good to have them back.'

Returning to that very limited special time in late 2020 of supporters being allowed in, Wayne Rooney, England's record goalscorer and no stranger to the odd controversy in his playing career, was interim manager of the Derby County team that played at Millwall. It was the players' first match in front of fans for nine months and Rooney was looking forward to it, even though Millwall can be an intimidating place for visitors. 'It's great when fans are in and there is banter going on,' he said. 'I'm sure the players and I will hear everything that is being said and I expect I'll get a bit of stick.'

It turned out Rooney wasn't the story that day after all, as the anticipated taunting of him was overshadowed by a small section of the 2,000 fans booing when the players of both teams took the knee before the game to honour Black Lives Matter. There was an attempted justification offered up afterwards that the booing was a protest against the alleged politicisation of the BLM movement. But it scarred the day, and Millwall manager Gary Rowett told Sky Sports, 'Of course I am disappointed. The club does an enormous amount of work on anti-racism.' Rooney also offered up his view: 'To hear it was very disappointing and upsetting for a lot of people. The players had to put it to the back of their minds during the game but I'm sure it's something they were thinking about.' One fan was rather more blunt with his Twitter summing-up: 'They are a disgrace. A select few chosen to return ... and this is how they use that privilege. Absolutely disgusting.'

Former England defender Micah Richards, who became a successful football pundit after his playing career, also wanted to know how tickets were allocated. He said on the BBC, 'There are 2,000 so you can pinpoint the people going. There are no excuses. I am sick to death of talking about this situation. We have come so far but we have so far to go. I don't even like talking about the matter. It feels like it falls on deaf ears. It is time and time and time again.'

Fellow pundit Dion Dublin, who had a loan spell as a Millwall player in 2002, added, 'They don't agree with taking the knee, which means they are racist. It says to me that a minority of Millwall fans are spoiling it for a club that is going in the right direction.'

It was by no means the last word on the subject but QPR players had the perfect response a few nights later when Millwall had another home match. They took the knee in celebration of an equalising goal, and the gesture was this time greeted with silence. As was their goal, of course.

Booing was also heard when players knelt on the ground before Colchester United's 2-1 win over Grimsby Town in front of around 1,000 spectators, and angry U's chairman Robbie Cowling said those fans were no longer welcome. Stay silent or stay away, he warned them. He said, 'For every game in future where the players choose to take the knee, I would like all of our fans to join me in applauding this gesture to ensure our players know we fully support them.'

So, football returned for what seemed like all of five minutes in front of a trickle of fans, but not without controversy. Everything had changed, yet nothing had changed there.

5

Nostalgia: Don't look back in anger

FOOTBALL NEEDS fans and fans need football. That much we learned from being kept away – for well over a year as it turned out. Premier League fans could watch all the matches on TV, as long as they had big wallets to get all the channels that were showing them. And they needed patient partners as it could take a marathon eight hours or so on a day of four back-to-back matches. For fans outside the top level, there was usually an opportunity to buy in matches of their favourite teams to watch at home. So that meant savings – in petrol or fares to get to and from the grounds and not having to buy actual tickets to watch an actual match.

But there's nothing like a live event, the colour, the atmosphere, the noise, the emotion, the camaraderie, the banter, the fun.

It's always been the same. Or has it? There were many pleasures that football used to bring us and we've learned to live without (for starters, what happened to rosettes?).

Here are just some of the things to be nostalgic about for those who've been football fans since back in the day. Well, the last century anyway.

Rattles

A fan probably wouldn't go to a match in, say, the 1950s without their rattle. But what were they all about? Made of wood with a handle and a mechanism that made a loud clacking noise when you swung it round, they were more practically used in the countryside as bird-scarers. The time to rattle your rattle was in celebration when your team had scored. But kids couldn't wait for that special occasion and used them throughout the match – probably rattling all the grown-ups nearby. A Liverpool fan's rattle specially painted red and white on the day of the 1950 FA Cup Final was recently exhibited at Anfield. The paint was apparently still wet as the late Len Tyrer carried it down Wembley Way to the match.

Standing on the terraces

You could choose your favourite spot to stand, and you wouldn't have to be next to someone you don't like, as can happen nowadays with numbered seats in the stand. All-seater stadiums, in the Premier League at least, have been compulsory since 1994 as a result of the Taylor Report into safety at football grounds following the Hillsborough disaster. For those who never got the chance, the experience of watching a big match while standing on a packed terrace was just something so exhilarating and exciting. And clearly unforgettable.

Crash barriers

When I was a boy, my dad liked getting to a ground early so we could get a crash barrier to either sit on or lean on. I always thought it was safer just in front of a barrier as if there was a surge from behind down packed terraces, we would have been in danger of being crushed against the metal barrier. But what did I know? And, anyway, if it was that crowded, us kids used to get passed over the heads of fans to stand right at the front. Jammed up against the barrier all over again.

Hooliganism

Some fans nostalgically reminisce about the horrific and stupid days when hooliganism and violence was commonplace at football. Joining a firm, picking fights, invading 'ends', waiting for rival groups after games, the thrill of the unexpected, the fear of getting injured or arrested. Chatting on social media – and there's plenty of opportunities to be found there to discuss the 'good old days' – one fan in 2021 remembered: 'Those days were so exciting, the fear, adrenaline, and anticipation used to outweigh whatever happened on the pitch.'

3pm kick-offs

All the matches used to start simultaneously on a Saturday afternoon which made everything simpler for fans and easier to plan for. It meant for an away game anywhere in the country you could travel there in the morning and return home in the evening. No dawn alarms for a midday kick-off or arriving home after midnight when the game's been rescheduled for 7.45pm. Mind you, when we say 3pm, it was 3.15pm kick-offs to take in shift changes at potteries (Stoke City) and docks (Millwall) – though many thought this was also to fit in a last pint before pubs closed at 3pm to prepare for the evening session.

Leather footballs
With laces. A right pain for heading. And, of course, as we now know, downright dangerous as well.

Comics
Roy of the Rovers in *Tiger, Goal, Shoot!, Charles Buchan's Football Monthly*; they were all an important part of growing up for the football-mad youngster. *Soccer Star* was my personal favourite, and I loved those League Ladders with little tabs in club colours that you moved up and down on a Sunday morning after the previous day's results. You learned reading (such funny names, some of the clubs), geography (where the teams came from), and maths (positions for clubs with equal points were decided on goal average until the 1970s which meant dividing goals scored by goals conceded).

Half-time scores
A man in a long brown coat used to climb a ladder to a wooden scoreboard and hang the half-time scores on rusty nails. A 1-0; B 2-1, etc. Crafty, that, as you had to buy a programme to find out who A and B were. Later, it got much simpler when the half-time scores were read out over the PA, or when one of the crowd brought his transistor

radio with him and called out 'Arsenal have scored' so everyone around him knew.

First aiders

Does anyone else remember fans on the terraces all waving their white handkerchiefs in the air to ask for assistance for one of their number who'd suddenly been taken ill? Two St John Ambulance volunteers would leap from the bench where they were watching the match and trot round the touchline, trailing a stretcher behind them, and the crowd would part like the Red Sea to let them through to treat the poor stricken guy.

Here come the teams

The players used to run out on to the pitch in line, with the centre-half jumping in the air to do pretend headers, the goalkeeper volleying a ball aimlessly skywards, and the player at the back of the line pausing to have a final drag on his cigarette.

Saturday afternoon TV

The iconic *Saint and Greavsie* with loveable former stars Ian St John and Jimmy Greaves previewing that afternoon's games. Followed by *Grandstand* or Dickie Davies and the goals and results coming in on the vidiprinter or Ceefax.

And talking of TV, the magnificent day-long FA Cup Final coverage, right from the moment when the camera followed the players as they left their hotel to get on the coach for the trip to Wembley. I loved all that.

Postponements

With no social media and few telephones, you'd have to make the journey to the ground to find out if a match was going to be called off. Martin Kilner recalls driving from Huddersfield to Plymouth only to find his game was postponed, and then completing a same-day 650-mile round trip to go home again. Many fans made countless fruitless journeys to Old Trafford to watch Manchester United play Huddersfield in the third round of the FA Cup in 1963 – it was postponed 12 times before finally being played.

Peanuts

Not salted or honey-roasted, just peanuts. Still in their shells. Fans could buy them (for peanuts!) in little bags from stalls outside the ground and then drop the shells on the terraces. It made for a satisfying crunching sound as you deliberately trod on them when leaving the ground.

Saturday night football editions

All round the country, evening newspapers produced football editions about 5.30pm on a Saturday. Fans queued outside newsagents to await their arrival and all credit to the dedicated teams back in the office who produced them so quickly as soon as the matches finished.

Changing ends at half-time

You still see it in non-league football but fans used to do it all the time at much higher levels to be at the end the home team were attacking for both halves. My brother Geoff said he remembered it as 'an exercise in optimism'.

Lock-outs

Never mind lockdown, it used to be lock-outs that fans worried about. Ian remembers an FA Cup tie between Manchester United and Preston in 1966 when he and his mates couldn't get to Old Trafford their preferred three hours before kick-off because of school and then rush-hour traffic. When they finally got there they joined a long queue to the turnstiles but then heard the dreaded bell sounding to say the ground was full with 60,000 already inside. And that was 90 minutes before kick-off. With thousands of others he and his mates lurked outside the whole evening to listen to the crowd noise as United won 3-1.

Other things that were left behind in the 20th century: Streakers (whatever happened to them, and what were they all about anyway?). Queuing and paying hard-earned cash to grumpy men at rusty turnstiles which were hard to push and narrow to get through even for skinny people. Sitting on the grass round the edge of the pitch when the terraces got overloaded. Leaving five minutes from full time to get to the front of the queue for the bus home. Kids-only enclosures. Wet sponges used by trainers to treat all on-field injuries, including broken legs. Orange balls when pitches were covered in snow. Teenage girl cheerleaders with pom-poms and ra-ra skirts welcoming players on to the pitch in the 1990s. Clubcall premium phone lines before someone kindly invented the internet. Watching the final scores come in on TVs in shop windows if you were unlucky enough to be out shopping on a Saturday afternoon.

A Facebook page called 'Lost Football Grounds and Terraces of the UK' hits the nostalgic note full on. One recent post asked about the difference between the comparatively new Emirates and the old Highbury. Arsenal fan Simon responded, 'I miss Highbury, proper football stadium. It's not about comfort, it's about football and singing on the terraces.' Martin commented, 'I loved it, fantastic ground with a fantastic atmosphere. My last trip there, all the toilets at one end were blocked except for one and hundreds of us waiting to use it. It was carnage. Brilliant memories.'

It never previously occurred to me that blocked toilets smelled of better times, golden days when the sun always shone and our team always won. Or that hooliganism, a subject that will inevitably have to be returned to in a bit more gory detail later in this book, should be looked back on with such sentimental affection. Another thread on that Facebook page discussed whether people had fallen out of love with the game because of higher prices to get in, foreign owners, play-acting footballers, and the dreaded VAR. Quite a few said how they much preferred the days gone by when it cost less, they were able to stand on the terraces, and the players seemed to passionately care about their clubs. Rose-tinted spectacles and all that.

More than 20 years ago, Dan Goldstein in the *1999/2000 Rough Guide to English Football*, put nostalgia into a completely different perspective: 'The "good old days" meant decrepit grounds; non-existent facilities for the young, the old, and the disabled; tedious route-one football; and a climate of fear and loathing engendered by persistent hooliganism.'

Will Hoon, in the book *Football Days*, had this to say on the debate: 'The transformation Italia '90 had on the status of English football cannot be understated – irony and humour replaced violence and intolerance. A raft of government legislation, along with CCTV and the revamping of many of the country's stadiums, combined to create a different fan culture.'

The perceived threat of hooliganism hung around, though, and Derick Allsop described in his book *Kicking in the Wind* a 1995 trip into Chesterfield on board the Rochdale supporters' club coach for an Auto Windscreen Trophy match: 'A police outrider came out to escort this presumably vulnerable or dangerous cargo of humanity – those on board accepted it as a legacy of a lunatic age which no one dared to pronounce was over.'

The transformation was undoubtedly taking place, though not as yet for Rochdale fans, and it was highlighted by Liverpool supporter Kevin Sampson in his laugh-a-minute book *Extra Time*. He said of a trip to Spurs in 1998, 'This is another of those used-to-be-lairy grounds that you can't get used to in its new, friendly guise. To a shameless coward like me, the walk up from Seven Sisters tube used to be the longest, most nerve-wracking hike to any league ground anywhere. Mobs of slobbering hooligans would emerge from side streets, bouncing up and down, dying for a row. Today, the side streets are full of BMWs and merchandise sellers while the hooligans are selling match tickets for £120 a pair.'

6

Starting young: Stairway to heaven

IF THE question is when did it all begin, then the answer is at a very early age. Around seven years old, hopefully your dad will have taken you to your first football match (incidentally, it's nearly always seven. You're too young at six and past it at eight). Once there, you're captivated by the noise, the atmosphere, the passion. One or two more such outings – at most – and you'll be a fan hooked for life.

This is how the late great England manager Sir Bobby Robson explained it: 'What is a football club? Not the buildings or the directors or the people who are paid to represent it. It's not the television contracts, get-out clauses, marketing departments or executive boxes. It's the noise, the passion, the feeling of belonging, the pride in your city. It's a small boy clambering up stadium steps for the very first time, gripping his father's hand, gawping at that hallowed stretch of turf beneath him, and, without being able to do a thing about it, falling in love.'

Many fans follow a particular club because it's a family tradition. If you live in Burnley, say, or Swansea, then your hometown club is going to become your team. For better or worse, for a lifetime. I was brought up in south London, and we had a choice of three clubs a bus ride away: Millwall, Charlton and Crystal Palace. We used to go to all of them, and when I got to my teens, to Spurs or Arsenal as well on dedicated double-deckers for football fans only, which took us to the grounds from New Cross bus garage. But really we grew up as Millwall supporters because that was my dad's team from his boyhood around the Old Kent Road. And his dad's before him – he remembered being taken by his sports-mad father to his first Millwall match as a kid and how they beat Luton 7-0. What a start to your footballing life.

We all have stories of our earliest memories as a supporter, and Robert Plant was mad on football from a very young age after Billy Wright waved to him. The lead singer and lyricist of rock band Led Zeppelin, Plant had been taken by his dad to watch his local club, Wolves. He recalled in an interview with his local paper, the *Express & Star*, 'Honest, he did. Billy Wright waved at me and I was hooked from that moment.'

Wright was a local hero, but he was more than that, too. He played for Wolves all his club career in the 1940s and '50s and was the first footballer in the world to win 100 international caps, in an age when England didn't play anything like as many games as now. He was also the David Beckham of his time – not for taking stunning free kicks or scoring from his own half, but for marrying a pop star. He wed Joy Beverley of the popular singing trio the

Beverley Sisters, and they were together for 36 years before Billy died of cancer in 1994.

Billy Wright was a CBE and so too is Robert Plant, who enjoyed a tremendous career as the archetypal rock-god singer and was voted 'the greatest voice in rock' in a radio station poll. His love of football continued all through his successful life in music, and in 2014 Wolves invited him to be a vice-president. He combined two of his great loves when he got on stage at the club's end-of-season awards night a few years later and, trademark long locks flowing, belted out 'Whole Lotta Love'.

In an interview with the music magazine *Record Collector*, Plant admitted that his love of football 'played havoc with his marriage'. For instance, it took him three days to get home to the Midlands from Wembley after Wolves won the 1974 League Cup Final. He said in the piece, 'It's the love of something where I don't have to be explaining myself, justifying it; being a spook on the edge. I'm right in the middle of it, and I love it to death. And it's right and it's wrong and it's banal. It's a panacea for me. I used to go to the South Bank in the early '70s, and I'd be there with 15,000 other people chain-smoking Woodbines, and I was just getting over the fact that if I went to some other place on the planet, I would have to have security. But instead of that, I was on somebody else's shoulders, falling through the crowd.' What a man, what a life.

The agony of being a committed fan from early childhood weighed very heavily with broadcaster, presenter and writer Adrian Chiles. He's been a passionate West Bromwich Albion supporter since his grandad took him to his first match when he was seven. He told *The Guardian* in an interview, 'As a kid, it caused me so much pain when we lost that I vividly recall looking forward to growing up, when it surely would not feel as bad. To my shame and discredit, it has got worse.'

In his book published in 2007, *We Don't Know What We're Doing*, Chiles talked candidly about his obsession with the Baggies – and that of many other West Brom fans he interviewed. Among their many stories, he tells of one woman who'd been watching them all her life and never seen them concede a goal. Mind you, she had a system which meant shutting her eyes every time the other team looked like they might score.

Before he was signed by Liverpool, England international Jamie Carragher was an Everton fan, devoted from an early age and following in his dad's footsteps. He writes in his book *The Greatest Games*, 'The game gripped me as a kid and never let go. Obviously, I had no idea I would become a professional footballer. Had I not, I would still be travelling home and away with my mates from Bootle to watch Everton.' Talking of support in the city for both clubs, there was a lovely picture at the 1986 all-Merseyside FA Cup Final of a dad all decked out in Liverpool red with his little daughter on his shoulders wearing the blue kit of Everton.

Going back to childhood, and no matter how long ago yours was, hands up if you never hopped off school, even just the once, to watch a football match?

Now a journalist with *The Times*, Gregor Robertson was a 14-year-old pupil at school in Edinburgh when

Scotland played Brazil in the opening game of the 1998 World Cup in France. In a lovely little story, he recalled, 'At assembly, the headteacher warned anyone thinking of skipping school to watch the match on TV that afternoon would be disciplined. "Don't even think about it," he said. It was a nice try. When the lunchtime bell rang a few hours later, there was a stampede of feet like a herd of wildebeest on the Serengeti. Children poured out of the school gates. Miss a minute of Scotland v Brazil. Aye, that'll be right.'

Happy days for talkSPORT's Tony Incenzo when he reported on QPR's home game with Stoke City in December 2020. He said kicking off at an odd time reminded him of 1974 when the miners' strike meant matches had to start early so they could be completed in daylight. Tony remembers, 'I bunked off school to meet my uncle Sean to go and see a game.' His first time at QPR was just before that and in 2015 he worked out he had seen every single first-team match at Loftus Road there ever since – league and cup, as well as friendlies and testimonials. He said, 'I've been going for 39 years and I hope I'll be there for another 39. I can't see a reason for it ever ending.'

Then there was Sheffield Wednesday in 1972 and the choice was pretty simple for one man. Fergus told the story online about his dad's option of going to school the same as every other day, or choosing to see the mighty Pelé play at Hillsborough. The legend was part of a money-spinning exercise by his Brazilian club Santos to play friendlies in many different countries in front of big crowds. In the Hillsborough match, Wednesday's Tommy Craig apparently spent the last ten minutes man-marking

Pelé so he could be next to him when the final whistle went and he would be head of the queue to request his shirt. The match had a 2.30pm kick-off, also because of a miners' strike which disrupted a lot of football – and life – in the 1970s. But 37,000 fans still managed to get there, including Fergus's dad, who had indeed made the naughty decision to bunk off school so he could tell everyone for the rest of his life that he'd seen Pelé play. While watching the match who did he bump into but his deputy headmaster. 'They both agreed,' said Fergus, 'not to tell the headmaster about each other!'

We all believe that sneaking out of school to see a football match is pretty daring, but it happened right back in the 19th century, though then it was work, not school. On the day Aston Villa beat Everton in the FA Cup Final to clinch the double in 1896/97, dozens of Birmingham factories had to abandon their Saturday morning shifts because thousands skived off work. The crowd of 65,000 at the final at Crystal Palace was a record at the time for any football match.

It's hardly rock-and-roll of Robert Plant and Billy Wright proportions, but my own football fandom started early in my life with me and my brother taking a bus ride to the magnificent open space that is Blackheath in south London. During the winter, 28 full-size football pitches were marked out there, all tucked in together, back to back and side by side. It was the sort of place where the Sunday footballers had to carry their own goalposts and erect them, the lightest player on the tallest player's shoulders to tie the top of the post to the crossbar. The tall player – he had to be strong as well – then walked slowly along the goal line with the bloke on his shoulders holding the bar horizontally until he could complete the job of erecting the goal at the other end. We never did see what would happen if the knots weren't strong enough to hold the bar intact when a ball was thudded against it.

Proper warm-ups didn't exist then, so ten players, all with their hands down their shorts to keep everything warm, stood around hitting random shots at a goalkeeper who'd never wanted to be the goalie in a Sunday football team anyway. My brother and I came into our own, racing to retrieve the footballs which inevitably were fired high, wide and handsome. The team we followed every week were called Evelina, and wore black and white stripes. That much I remember but little else, except that every time a referee gave a sharp blast of his whistle, then play would immediately stop on about six adjoining pitches as well.

At the end of a game we'd pick a different player each week to ask, 'Where are you playing next week?' Football groupies that we were, we'd even be thrilled at the almost inevitable reply of 'Dunno, son.'

As well as our Sunday morning Blackheath jaunts, likely as not the previous afternoon would have seen us at Millwall. Of all the sights and sounds at the much-loved old Den, I remember especially at least 60 fans climbing a floodlight pylon to get a great view of the match. An official attendance of 45,646 had squeezed in to see the Lions play mighty Newcastle in a 1957 FA Cup tie. Bet your life that there were a few thousand more than that, and the fact that 50 supporters fainted that day confirms it was all pretty congested. The fans up the pylon got a super view, but how dangerous it must have been, especially in the excitement of Millwall scoring twice to win the game. And what about if the bloke at the top needed a pee at half-time? Surely it would never be allowed to happen again, and as I recall, roll upon roll of barbed wire prevented just that.

And yet in 2017, about 100,000 fans got into a stadium with an official capacity of 78,000 in Tehran to see a World Cup qualifier between Iran and China. And many of them made the perilous climb up the floodlight pylons that day, too, to get an uninterrupted view. Even more dramatic than the pictures of those fans up pylons was a tremendous black-and-white photograph of the crowd at Leicester's Filbert Street ground for an FA Cup tie with Spurs in 1928. Up to 1,000 fans in an overpacked stadium were sat perched together on the roof of the stand behind one of the goals. It looked really dangerous, but exhilarating too.

Talking of Millwall, back in those days when everything seemed pure and innocent, one fan was a train driver, and by complete coincidence just happened to be on the very line that went past the old Den on a Saturday afternoon soon after matches started. He had a terrific vantage point to stop and watch for a while before moving on, his restart leaving behind a huge plume of belching smoke which enveloped half the crowd and two-thirds of the pitch. That would have been familiar to fans of amateur Slovakian club TJ Tatran Čierny Balog who have to stand up to continue watching a match whenever a train goes by. That's because a narrow gauge railway line actually runs between the stand and the pitch. Not only does a train going through block their view but there's the steam from its chimney to contend with as well. A short video of a train passing a match while fans clapped it on its way went viral in 2015 and is well worth catching up with online.

7

Families: Back home they'll be thinking about us

RETIRED FOOTBALLER Andy McCall was happily sitting in the stand enjoying the celebrations as Bradford City were awarded the Third Division trophy at their final match of the season, at home to Lincoln on 11 May 1985. His son Stuart, who later became the club's manager as well as a Scotland international, was out on the pitch immersed in the game when a fire suddenly took hold in the stand where Andy was. It spread rapidly and fiercely, killing 56 fans who couldn't escape in time, and injuring hundreds of others, including McCall senior.

As soon as they could, Stuart and his brother drove to the nearest hospital to find out about their dad. Once there, they were horrified to be told the more seriously injured had already been transferred to a bigger hospital 15 miles away. Andy had survived but suffered 25 per cent burns to his body. Stuart returned to the hospital a couple of days later with the championship trophy to show it to his dad and the other fans who'd been injured and were still on the ward. He was worried that parading the silverware could seem a pretty trite gesture up against the human tragedy that had taken place. But the sight of the trophy had a unifying effect, reminding the fans of what had brought them together in the first place that fateful afternoon. Andy was in hospital for several weeks but recovered and lived to the grand old age of 89.

Footballers everywhere acknowledge who their number one fans are. Their mums and dads, the first people in their lives to kick a ball around with them, and the ones who regularly ferried them to and from training when they attracted the attention of a big club. They're the ones who've been their most loyal fans – and probably the most critical – as they've built careers in the game.

Luton Town's Sonny Bradley had fantastic support from his dad, Ray, and he was devastated to lose him in December 2020 after he'd contracted Covid-19. Ray was only 57 and very well known and popular with the Luton fans.

Sonny told BBC Radio 5 Live, 'My dad was a great man. If I could have picked anyone on the planet to be my dad I would have chosen him. He was my biggest fan and I got a lot from him, especially when it came to football. After games it hit me the hardest as everyone has someone to turn to and get things off their chest. Everywhere I've been he was probably the first to arrive, mixing with the fans and getting involved with the spirit of the club.' Poignantly, after his dad died, Sonny asked that everyone at the club should just treat him as normal. 'Deep down, behind the mask, I was hurting,' he added, 'but when I'm at football I'm busy and my mind is occupied.'

Like Bradley, West Ham's Saïd Benrahma was very keen to resume playing as soon as he could after the death of his father. He was at Brentford at the time, and after scoring in a match in 2020 he revealed a T-shirt with the message 'I love you, dad'. His manager Thomas Frank said, 'He's had some emotional days but he said he wanted to play for his dad.'

As with many footballers all over the world, David Beckham recognised the crucial part his dad played in his illustrious career. In his book *My Side*, Beckham wrote, 'My dad was the original Cockney Red. And he passed the passion on to me even before I knew he was doing it. Dad was ten years old at the time of the 1958 Munich air crash. He had already been following Manchester United but the disaster turned it into a lifelong obsession for him. I think it was the same for a lot of supporters of his generation.'

While Beckham's dad was a driving force in getting him into United colours when lots of other clubs already knew of his potential, other fathers have been role models in players taking up professional careers. Kasper Schmeichel, Frank Lampard, Darren Ferguson (he got sold by his dad Alex from Manchester United to Wolves for £250,000) and Erling Haaland are among many sons who have followed their fathers into the game. And former Manchester City and England player Mike Summerbee had both a dad and a son who played professionally. Three generations of footballers.

In the heat of a game it's easy for fans to occasionally forget that no matter how top clubs might protect them from reality, players are just the same as them underneath – ordinary people with everyday problems. And with families who love them.

There was a great deal of sympathy for Spurs and England defender Eric Dier when he saw his brother embroiled in a heated argument with a fan after a particularly disappointing home defeat in March 2020 in an FA Cup tie. A clearly wound-up Dier climbed up over empty seats in the stands to intervene. He had to be held back by his brother, stewards and other fans to prevent a verbal row possibly turning into a physical one before the abuser made a pretty swift exit. Spurs manager José Mourinho said, 'When someone insults you and your family is involved, Eric did something we would all do. But we as professionals cannot do what he did.' The FA agreed and suspended Dier for four matches and fined him £40,000.

Now a happier little story – all one particular dad wanted to do was protect his family while watching his six-year-old playing in a game in Wales. The lad was in goal and when he didn't react to a shot coming in from the wing that was on target, dad pushed him over in front of the ball, and the lad's fallen body blocked the shot. Unfortunately for the enthusiastic father the laugh-out-loud moment was captured on video, and at the last count 18 million people had seen what happened in this under-eights match. 'I was just trying to guide him back to position when he fell over,' explained the loving parent.

Spurs fan John Connolly has his mum to thank for his love of the club. He tweeted, 'When I was four I needed a PE kit (white shirt and navy shorts) as I was starting primary school. Mum came back with the Spurs 1981 cup winners' shirt – I didn't look back from that day.'

A loyal Liverpool fan, Colin, posted about his love of Anfield on social media and of its place in his family history: 'This has been my family's home ground since at least 1918 with my grandad, my dad, me and my sons all walking up to the ground. The thought of ever moving to a soulless bowl fills me with fear and I'm so glad this will forever be my and my family's footballing home.' Mind you, Dean charmingly responded to the post: 'A hole with restricted views! An over-hyped artificial atmosphere started by playing a crap song.'

Colin's story reminded me of the day I popped into a computer shop to get my laptop looked at. The owner and I recognised one another as club cricketers who'd often played against each other. I didn't remind him that I once hit a rare six off his bowling – I still remember the comforting thwack as the ball bounced on to a concrete path just beyond the admittedly very short leg-side boundary. Never mind cricket, we soon got on to the subject of football and it turned out Ron – Ron Brown to give him his name – was a Portsmouth season ticket holder. 'Do you know what's my favourite bit of the whole afternoon?' he asked. 'Walking down the road to the ground with my dad on one side of me and my son on the other. Three generations sharing the same love of football and Pompey.'

Ron would enjoy what Brazilian star Ronaldinho said about Portsmouth. When AC Milan played at Fratton Park in 2008 in the UEFA Cup, he was quoted as saying it had one of the 'best atmospheres in world football'. And much-loved Liverpool manager Bob Paisley said it was like an away game at Anfield in the 1980s when 16,000 rowdy Portsmouth fans were packed in at one end. Jamie commented in a Facebook reminiscence about that day, 'When it was goalless the Pompey fans were going crazy with songs like "0-0 to the team in blue". Then Liverpool scored four but they still didn't stop singing. Great fans.'

I'm not sure all Portsmouth fans would be pleased with his description of their town, but the sentiments from Barnsley's ex-Pompey striker Conor Chaplin were nice. He said, 'What I love about the two clubs I've played for are the fans. At working-class places like that, people want hard work and graft and that's what I believe in as well.'

8

Fanatics: We'll support you evermore

THE WORD 'fan' means 'enthusiast, supporter' and is simply a short form of 'fanatic'. That in turn derives from the Latin word 'fanaticus' which means 'inspired by God'. While we're on the subject of words, groups of fans in Italy are called 'tifosi' – 'those infected by typhus' – as their fanaticism is likened to someone acting as if they have a fever.

Sounding for all the world like the Incredible Hulk, one particular 'fanaticus' is John Westwood, who by day is a seller of antique and second-hand books and by night (well, on Tuesday nights and Saturday afternoons anyway) he transforms into a fanatical football fan. Not just any fan, but one of the most recognisable and famous supporters in the UK.

John Anthony Portsmouth Football Club Westwood – he changed his name by deed poll in 1989 – has about 60 Portsmouth tattoos, and additionally has PFC engraved on his teeth. He has the club crest shaved on to his head, covered at matches by a curly blue wig and outrageously large hat, and rings the 'Pompey Chimes' on a handbell repeatedly throughout. *Match of the Day* cameras loved to get him in close-up back in Pompey's Premier League days. Artist Karl Rudziak, who painted John for the BP Portrait Awards exhibition at the National Portrait Gallery in London, said the tattoos and costumes were not exhibitionism. They were John's way, he explained, of externalising his deep passion for Portsmouth FC as well as reflecting his inner self.

While doing his day job, as a partner in the family's bookshop business in Petersfield, Hampshire, John covers up his tattoos. And when he goes to a book fair he puts on a suit but invariably ends up talking about football and his tats anyway. In January 2020, a tweet that he'd posted saying he'd not had any customers in the bookshop that day went viral and he ended up overwhelmed with online orders. He said one man came into the shop the next day for the first time, even though he'd lived in the town all his life, and said, 'My friend who lives in San Francisco heard about you and told me I had to come in.'

My favourite ever football book, *Playing at Home* by John Aizlewood, is about how he watched matches at all 92 Premier League and Football League grounds during the 1997/98 season – a dream to start with that ended as a logistical and often depressing nightmare. But it was hilarious and beautifully written, too. Anyone who's ever been lonely watching a match on their own, let alone one just to tick off yet another game at yet another ground, will relate to this. It's a Tuesday evening in January with Notts County playing Hull and the first half has been awful. John writes in the book, 'There's nobody within ten rows of me in any direction. I'm beset by the sharp stabbing pains I get in my guts when I think of fitting in another 35 games before 11 May and I'm so cold I've lost all feeling in my feet. Behind the goal are the 60 or so travelling Hull fans and now they're restless. They notice me and start to chant, louder than I thought it possible for 60 people to chant, as they point at me, "What's it like, what's it like, what's it like to have no friends?" I don't respond, other than slumping further down my slippery plastic seat. I haven't the heart. It's awful having no friends. I am the loneliest man in the world.'

Another fan of visiting all 92 professional grounds was university lecturer Simon Henig, who completed that challenge in 1995. Since then, he has been going to all the newly built stadiums – and newly promoted clubs – to keep his list bang up to date. His personal rule is that he must see a competitive match at any new ground and he's now visited 146 different English clubs, as well as more than 100 in non-league, and is working his way through all the Scottish league.

A similar sort of commitment was shown by Steve Hill, who decided to watch every Chester City match, home and away, throughout a whole season. Such an accomplishment is called *The Card* and he got a superb book out of it, the highs and lows of a season on the road, all 15,000 miles of it. A lovely story of the many Steve tells is of him desperately wanting his team, Chester, not to get an equaliser in a cup tie because it would mean a midweek replay. That in turn would have meant faffing about making after-school arrangements, another huge road trip, and another long-after-midnight bedtime to maintain the commitment he'd made to seeing every minute of every match.

Talking of loyal fans, one supporter of Argentinian club Boca Juniors said on his deathbed that his last wish was to be wrapped in a flag of hated rivals River Plate so that when he died it would look as if they'd lost one of their own. The story is told by renowned Uruguayan writer Eduardo Galeano in his book *Soccer in Sun and Shadow*. He points out a man can change his wife, his politics or his religion, but he can't change his favourite football team. Galeano then changes tack with another thought: 'I go about the world, hand outstretched, and plead, "A pretty move, for the love of God." And when good soccer happens, I give thanks for the miracle and I don't give a damn which team or country performs it.'

Another pretty fanatical fan got in the face of Republic of Ireland international Eamon Dunphy while he was playing for Millwall. He recalled the moment in his book, *Only a Game?*: 'I was walking off the pitch when I caught the eye of this big fat guy who stands just beside the tunnel. He goes to reserve games, everything. I've seen him all over the country. He seems really aggressive. I've never spoken to him but I don't like him. I caught his eye and he gave me the old wanking sign. Contempt.' And that was from one of his own fans; imagine what it must have been like for the opposition players when they walked by.

By coincidence, Dunphy was in the Reading team when it was champagne all round as they won promotion from the old Fourth Division in 1975/76. The players left the bubbly behind in the dressing room for a bit as they went back out after the game to celebrate with their fans and throw their shirts to them. But the supporters wouldn't leave until manager Charlie Hurley came out to acknowledge them. 'You're the people we do it for,' he told them in a story recorded by Paul McGuigan and Paolo Hewitt in their book, *The Greatest Footballer You Never Saw*, about mercurial striker Robin Friday. What short memories. Earlier that very same season Hurley was quoted in the book as saying about the fans, 'What I think about them is unprintable.'

That was after they had hummed the 'Death March' during a home match with Huddersfield. 'If they want us to play kick and rush,' raged Hurley, 'that's the best way to invite defeat.'

We know he was being flippant, but the actor Stephen Mangan, a Spurs season ticket holder, commented on social media in 2020, 'I can't deal with lockdown AND Spurs playing like this. We need to suspend all football indefinitely!' Mangan reckons he first took his son to a Spurs match when the boy was an eight-day-old baby – I wonder what the nearby fans thought of that. He told *The Guardian* in an interview in 2008, 'Spurs is a frustrating club to support but it's never boring at the Lane. Arsenal have spent less money than us, they've got a beautiful new stadium, they're vastly more successful – but they're weird and wrong. Who'd want to be them?'

There's loyalty to your favourite football team – and then there was Norman Windram. A lifelong Manchester United fan, he claimed in 2002 to have been at every home match at Old Trafford since 1926. He said his dad had taken him to his first game – against Oldham – at the tender age of four and he then saw nearly 2,000 more in a row. Norman died in 2009 at the age of 87.

Talking of fans taking it all very seriously, my enjoyment of a match I was watching wasn't really spoiled by overhearing the second-half conversation between two 'old boys'. Well, they were both a bit deaf and shouted loudly at each other so I couldn't help but catch every word. 'He's picked the wrong team,' said one. 'Yes, he doesn't know what he's doing,' his friend replied. And the moaning went on between them. 'And his tactics are wrong.' 'Yes, he needs someone else up front.' 'And the players can't pass the ball.' 'Or head it.' 'They should shoot when they get the chance.' 'It's the worst we've been all season.' 'And that's saying something.' So it went on, a non-stop depressed moanathon for the whole 45 minutes. And at the end of the game? 'They're at home again on Tuesday evening.' 'Yes, see you then.' 'Yes, see you Tuesday, mate.'

Nick Hornby sums up beautifully the depressed attitude of so many fans in his seminal football book *Fever Pitch*: 'What impressed me most was just how much most of the men around me hated, really hated, being there. As far as I could tell, nobody seemed to enjoy, in the way that I understood the word, anything that happened during the entire afternoon. Within minutes of the kick-off there was real anger ("You're a DISGRACE, Gould. He's a

DISGRACE!" "A hundred quid a week? A HUNDRED QUID A WEEK! They should give that to me for watching you."); as the game went on, the anger turned into outrage, and then seemed to curdle into sullen, silent discontent. Yes, yes, I know all the jokes. What else could I have expected at Highbury? But I went to Chelsea and to Tottenham and to Rangers, and saw the same thing: that the natural state of the football fan is bitter disappointment, no matter what the score.'

There was a wonderful example of a fan's obsessive pessimism in a special edition of the *Cambridge Evening News* in 1978, celebrating Cambridge United's second successive promotion. They'd just finished runners-up in the old Third Division, having won the Fourth Division the previous season, and this after only getting into the Football League eight years earlier. One particular fan made regular weekly calls to the club's vice-chairman Tony Douglas, who jotted down the unsolicited advice he was being given!

'August: No goals against Brighton and Bradford. No chance of keeping up unless some forwards are purchased.

'September: Nice to see you off the bottom at last. Lucky against Plymouth – own goal, I see. Colchester and Exeter are doing well – thought they were both better sides than you last season.

'October: Preston and Wrexham put you in your place. Win against Swindon a flash in the pan.

'November: Team looked terrible on TV against Peterborough. Look like having a mid-table position by the end of the season.

'December: Poor cup result against Plymouth which will probably react with poor league results.

'January: Was coming to see the Peterborough match but couldn't get a stand ticket. Ought to improve your ground for next season. Can't see any success now with your manager departing [Ron Atkinson went to West Bromwich Albion].

'February: These two managers will do you no good at all. Get someone like [former Chelsea boss Eddie] McCreadie. Lucky against Preston, it didn't look like a penalty on TV. The slide now appears to be on the way.

'March: Too many team changes. To lose at both Rotherham and Colchester will mean Third Division again next season. Be a good thing as you're not Second Division material.

'10 April: What went wrong at Lincoln? Club now shot its bolt. You'll be lucky to get five points from your remaining four matches.

'24 April: Touch and go now. If only you had beaten Lincoln. Team playing too defensive, I understand, to get four points in the remaining two games.

'2 May: [Cambridge have won their two remaining games and are promoted] Congratulations on going up. Thought all along that you might do it. Unless you get some new players you won't last long in the Second Division, though. Might come along and see you regularly next season, I only saw four matches this season.'

Most of all I love the comment when he said he always thought Cambridge would be going up! The thing is we all know fans who are always looking on the negative side and I absolutely believe these are genuine comments that the vice-chairman noted whenever he called.

To be a true fan you've got to be able to take defeat on the chin. It comes with the territory; losing is very much part of the experience. Self-deprecating humour helps and possibly being a pessimist – there's no point going to every game thinking your team are going to win. They ain't. Perhaps the words on this birthday card will assist, 'On his birthday he reflected on the tears of desperation, the almost unimaginable loneliness and the heartfelt yearning for something better … still maybe that was the price you paid for supporting a shite football club.'

Tweeting helps as well. These were a couple of heartfelt examples during the 2020/21 season:

Matt: 'It's really hard to believe * [name removed to protect the innocent] were once a team that challenged for titles. No effort from the players, owner, or the club. Seems only the fans care about the club now, and it shows in the recent fortunes of the club.' * Okay, all right, it was Newcastle.

Will: 'This might be the worst side * have ever had in the Premier League. And there have been some pretty terrible ones over the last 20 years.' * Okay, this was West Brom.

It's nice when an insult gets turned into a much-loved nickname by fans. Twenty years ago Ipswich were winning 2-1 against Leeds, whose fans started chanting, 'We're being beaten by a bunch of tractor drivers.' Rather than being offended at the barb at their agricultural heritage, Ipswich's fans turned it on themselves and began calling themselves the Tractor Boys. Former manager Jim Magilton complained that it conjured up images of carrot-crunching yokels. Yup, but that's the way it is now.

Actually, he looked far from happy about it, but Burnley fan and BBC Radio 1 presenter Jordan North thought only of football when he had to do a fearsome bushtucker trial on *I'm a Celebrity…Get Me Out of Here!* in 2020. He explained, 'My brother, who is a paratrooper, said to me no matter how scared or cold you get, to think of your happy place.' For Jordan, that meant Burnley's Turf Moor ground, and while surrounded by snakes – his worst fear – he kept shouting 'happy place, happy place, Turf Moor, Turf Moor'. He admitted, 'That's the most terrifying thing I've ever done in my life.'

9

Jokers: Feeling glad all over

DON'T WE all just love a good banner at a football ground to demonstrate the wit and wisdom of fans. Here's a few from over the years:

'He's not the Messiah, he's a very naughty boy' – aimed by Burnley fans at Owen Coyle who had been 'God' when he managed their club, but 'Judas' when he switched to Bolton.

'I am incandescent with rage (but I'm British so I'm just holding a sign)' – nice tongue-in-cheek message among the angry banners protesting about the proposed European Super League.

'£64 a ticket'– Bayern Munich fans have a pop at how much it cost to watch their team at Arsenal. Other banners completed the message: 'But without fans football is not worth a penny.'

'The Chosen One' – in honour of David Moyes when he took over as Manchester United manager in 2013. 'The Wrong One' appeared when his job there lasted for only ten months.

'They've got Xavi and Pirlo but we've got Long-Cox' – Republic of Ireland fans at Euro 2012 celebrate having Shane Long and Simon Cox in their squad.

'You told us to come back when we've won 18 … We are back' – Manchester United supporters respond to Liverpool taunts after winning their 18th league title in 2009.

'C'Mon Chels GR8 T B Back' – someone spent lockdown creating this Chelsea banner.

'Stay safe. Support us at home' – another lockdown message, this time at Liverpool.

'Win draw or lose we Kane forever the booze' – Spurs fans drink to Harry Kane's health.

'Goodbye to our history for nothing' – West Ham's faithful protest at leaving Upton Park.

'Created by the poor, stolen by the rich' – supporters protest about plans for a European Super League.

'Crawley Town FC this love will last forever' – nothing more to be said.

'A man can love many women, but only one club' – Bayer Leverkusen fans set to be banished to the spare room when they got home after putting up that one.

No book about the fun of being a football supporter would be complete without an inflatable banana or two. Unusually for a craze, as they normally creep up on us when we're not looking, we can identify exactly where this one began. It was on the terraces at Manchester City in August 1987 at a time when football was at a pretty low ebb as a result of hooliganism, tragedies and disasters at matches. Not to mention the political wrangling about what should be done about it all.

A City fan called Frank Newton started it. He'd seen a five-foot inflatable banana in a friend's toy collection and was allowed to borrow it, provided he could supply the necessary photographic proof that he'd actually taken it to a game. So Frank paraded it at City's first match of the season, in August of that year against Plymouth, and got a mate to take a picture. He even drew a face and bobble hat on the banana to give it a bit of a personality, as it were.

He kept taking it to the ground and somehow the banana became associated with City player Imre Varadi who must have been thrilled to earn the nickname of 'Imre Banana'. Though as he uses it more than 30 years later on his Twitter handle he can't have been that put out. Shops in Manchester began to stock supplies of inflatable bananas to meet a growing demand, and there were bunches of them turning up on the terraces. Perish the thought, but they were even seen at Lancashire's county cricket matches the following summer.

The fun spread the following football season, and more and more clubs were at it. Manchester City fans were still at the forefront and, like it or not, it wasn't just bananas. There were still hundreds of them but fans also took a crocodile to one match as well as a toucan, a seven-foot golf club, parrots, gorillas and a paddling pool that needed four lads to carry. At one match at West Bromwich there was a Godzilla and a Frankenstein's Monster whose play fight was more entertaining than the on-pitch action itself. In another game at Stoke, fans turned up in fancy dress and the club itself paid homage to the whole crazy craze as the

City players came out carrying inflatable bananas which they threw into the crowd.

For the return match at City, Stoke fans turned up with 3,000 Pink Panthers, and by then the inflatables mania had well and truly spread through football. Oldham fans brought inflatable dogs to games, West Ham inflatable hammers, Lincoln City fans waved inflatable penises after a rival club's chairman mistakenly tweeted a picture of his manhood, Bristol City fans had blow-up fangs in honour of manager Joe Jordan, Blackpool fans inflatable towers, and Grimsby fans an inflatable Harry Haddock fish.

The whole banana business died down, as such things do, but events took a bit of a wrong turn in 2009 when Sunderland beat Liverpool 1-0 with a Darren Bent goal that deflected off an inflatable beach ball which had been thrown on to the pitch. The teenage Liverpool fan who threw it subsequently received death threats and the referee was in hot water for allowing the goal, as under the laws an 'outside agent' on the pitch means the game should have been stopped immediately.

But the fad hadn't gone away completely and even in 2016 Everton goalkeeper Joel Robles was pictured removing an inflatable banana from the pitch during a League Cup semi-final with Manchester City at the Etihad.

And fishy Grimsby fans stayed loyal to Harry Haddock long after the movement had drowned out elsewhere and were banned as recently as 2017 from taking inflatables to a match at Barnet. Two years previously in a match there, fans had thrown beach balls and blow-up footballs on to the pitch and a fan was found guilty of assaulting a steward with an inflatable shark.

A good wind-up makes for a good day out, though perhaps not for the Dover Athletic fan who was the subject of it during an FA Cup third round tie at Huddersfield in January 2011. One supporter from each club was invited to take part in a penalty shoot-out with a twist on the pitch at half-time. The twist, which indeed it was, meant running quickly ten times round a spike in the ground before sprinting to kick the penalty into an empty net. Ever tried doing that? It's hard enough to stay on your feet at the end of ten quick giddy-inducing spins, let alone run off and kick a ball. The Huddersfield fan managed it, though, even if his sprint to the penalty spot was wobbly – it was almost as if he'd done it before! The Dover follower, on the other hand, hadn't. He stepped forward wearing a sparkling clean white sailor suit, even though his home town is better known for the ferries to Calais than any Royal Navy connections. The man with the mic started his countdown of spins. 'One, two, three, four, five, six, seven,' pause, 'three, four, five, six.' The poor lad was on about 16, and still counting, when he lost it completely and slithered sideways into the muddiest part of the pitch. Quite a coincidence that the home club had chosen that particular spot to do it. He tottered up, his pristine white suit covered in mud, and had to concede victory to Huddersfield. Just like his team did that day.

Whereas some footballers have been known to sneer about their fans – behind their backs, anyway – Garry Nelson didn't take them for granted. In his second book, *Left Foot in the Grave*, he fondly remembered going out for a pre-match warm-up at Barnet when he was player-coach of Torquay in 1996/97. Greeted by a chorus of 'Oh Garry, Garry, Garry, Garry, Garry Nelson' he immediately waved to the Torquay fans in the away end. Then he realised they'd been joined by a crowd of Charlton supporters who had gone along to add their support for one of their favourite former players. To have one lot of fans singing your name is nice, but to have two is, well, twice as good!

One of my favourite Nelson stories in that book is a Torquay match away to Bristol City early in the same season, when he was sent flying by a very late tackle. He looked up to see the perpetrator, City captain Martin Kuhl, glaring down at him. 'Who the hell d'you think you are writing things like that about me in your book?' Kuhl asked. Nelson, whose previously published book *Left Foot Forward* was a lovely insight into the life of a professional footballer, mused to himself, 'Skipper, and it seems, literary critic.'

That reminded me of a cricket match held between a team of local media people and Gillingham footballers and staff to celebrate the end of a successful season. One of the journalists went in to bat and faced the bowling of Gillingham's young (at the time) and aggressive centre-half, one Steve Bruce. The first ball Bruce bowled to him was twice as fast as any he'd previously delivered and bounced up to sizzle past dangerously close to his ears. And that was before cricket helmets were in common use. 'What's all that about?' said the sports editor, advancing down the pitch. 'It's only a friendly cricket match.' 'That,' said the bristling Bruce, 'will teach you to give me six out of fucking ten in your paper.'

Phil Smith was on holiday at the Italian lakes in 1999 and was there the night Manchester United played in the UEFA Champions League Final against Bayern Munich. Among others watching it on TV in the bar that memorable evening was John Aston's cousin. Yes, the same John Aston who'd played for United when they'd previously won the European Cup in 1968. John's cousin decided to nip to the toilet when United got their late equaliser against Bayern so he'd be all ready for extra time. The rest is history, of course, as while his back was turned United scored again to spark wild victory celebrations. Lovely story, and made all the more special when you look up John Aston's contribution to that 1968 final and see that, even as one of the lesser-known names in a star-studded United line-up, he was actually named man of the match that night for his performance in a 4-1 win over Benfica.

An ill-timed toilet break didn't happen only on that evening, though, as another fan nipped out just as one of the best and most significant goals of the last ten years was going in. This goal was scored from 30 yards by Vincent Kompany against Leicester at the end of the 2018/19 season and it was crucial for Manchester City as they went on to clinch the Premier League title. A clip of the fan walking out with his back to the game at just the moment Kompany scored his wonder strike went viral. And, of course, the poor fan had the piss mercilessly taken out of him for ever after.

Also the butt of relentless leg-pulling was the Southampton fan at a League Cup tie in 2019 against old rivals Portsmouth. He was searching in his pockets for his phone – we've all done it – while everyone around him was celebrating a goal in a 4-0 win. When he eventually found his mobile he still filmed himself doing his own little celebration long after everyone else had stopped. And fellow fans made sure they'd captured that moment with their own cameras to prolong his embarrassment.

Picture the scene: Arsenal supporters on the underground on their way to a match at the Emirates and none of them have any trousers on. Their top halves all look completely normal and properly dressed, but below that they're all in just shoes and socks. Oh, and underpants. Like many a good craze, it came straight from the States where a practical joke group calling themselves Improv Everywhere arranged a co-ordinated pants-only subway journey across New York. Those taking part were told the whole point was they must keep a straight face at all times. If anyone asked they should just tell people they'd not remembered to put on their trousers, and it must be just a coincidence that others had apparently forgotten theirs as well.

If you believed them you believed anything, but loyal fans were fooled by Manchester City jokers Sergio Agüero and Kevin De Bruyne when they apparently dropped the 2019 Premier League trophy off a balcony before a parade round the city. The club's chief executive officer Ferran Soriano seemed annoyed and banged on a window. But it was all a joke and the players had deliberately dropped a replica trophy to play an 'amusing' prank on watching fans.

With football supporters being the charming and amusing crowd we know them to be, it was no surprise they burst into song when one of their number proposed to his girlfriend on the pitch at half-time. 'Congratulations'? 'You're Getting Married in the Morning'? Well, no, they actually sang, 'You don't know what you're doing.' But groom-to-be Anthony Tomlinson took it in good heart. 'I thought it was very funny,' he said. Chef Anthony made his proposal during a Peterborough United home match in September 2017 when he asked his partner Yasmin to marry him. The club had set up a spoof Mr and Mrs competition and pretended the couple had been picked out at random to take part, which was all part of Anthony's secret plan. He told the *Peterborough Telegraph*, 'I went down on one knee and asked Yasmin to marry me and luckily she looked delighted and said yes straightaway. It was a great moment for us both and after my proposal the team started to play really well.'

Levi Stone went one better by arranging his actual wedding for the half-time break in a Premier League fixture – and on the pitch itself in front of 28,000 fans. The match was Stoke City against Spurs in 2013 and it was for the BBC Three show *Don't Tell the Bride*, which featured men organising weddings behind their partners' backs. The happy couple watched the match in their wedding gear from VIP seats and the only disappointment about the day for 23-year-old Stoke fan Levi was that his team lost. His fiancée Jade, who admitted to wondering what the hell she was doing at a football match on her wedding day, had to wear football boots for the ceremony so her high heels didn't damage the turf. But she said, 'I wanted to marry him wherever it would be and I wouldn't change any of it for the world.' Levi said, 'The ground is like my church so I thought it would be a perfect venue.' Before partying the night away with 150 guests on a specially laid dance floor on the pitch complete with goals and cardboard cut-out footballers.

It was football that united another couple in unexpected circumstances, as they met through the Facebook page of Germany international Lukas Podolski. Fernanda Santana Sontos added a comment on something Podolski, who was then at Arsenal, had posted. Her comment and picture were seen by Simon Hinsel and the couple were soon in touch with each other and friendship developed into something lasting. Podolski himself was quoted in *Metro*: 'I'm glad for being the cupid of this beautiful relationship. Enjoy your love and the rest of your lives.'

Another international footballer, ex-Everton and Republic of Ireland midfielder Kevin Sheedy, unwittingly played a key role in getting together a couple back home. When he scored against England in the 1990 World Cup, two strangers in a crowd watching on a big screen ended up hugging and kissing in celebration. One thing led to another and wedding bells followed. Sheedy told *The Echo* much later, 'I've had cats and dogs named after me but nobody had actually got married thanks to me, so that was good.'

The last word on football-related weddings goes to the fan who posted an advert in the *Yorkshire Evening*

Post before a crucial derby match: 'Man offers marriage proposal to any woman with ticket for Leeds United v Sheffield United game. Must send photograph (of ticket).'

10

Tragedies: You'll never walk alone

IT WASN'T straightforward to include a chapter about tragedies, disasters, hooliganism and racism in this book. This publication is mainly an entertaining, light-hearted look at what it's like to be a football fan, and how much pleasure it gives us. Those people who were involved in a lot of the loathsome hooligan stuff that beset the game, from the 1970s through the forgettable 1980s, aren't actually supporters at all – just hangers-on who were tagging along for the violence and vandalism. Blame society, not football, for what went on.

On the other hand, the people who lost their lives in the cruellest of tragedies in that decade, such as Hillsborough or Bradford, were genuine fans. They were there simply because they loved the game and wanted to go with friends to watch a football match. So in tracing back the history of the game and its fans, these stories have to be confronted and told. We've learned from them, and although we're nearly a quarter of the way through the following century already and things are still by no means perfect, we're better off now and far safer while watching the game we treasure.

Everyone over a certain age remembers where they were on 15 April 1989. I was watching a Southern League match and the PA announcer only gave the half-time score from one of the FA Cup semi-finals being played that afternoon. But not the other one, between Liverpool and Nottingham Forest. I wondered why, but these were the days before mobile phones and the all-seeing internet, so we knew nothing about the devastating tragedy of Hillsborough until we got home and put the television on.

We now know exactly what happened on that fateful day in Sheffield. Queues were building up outside the turnstiles at the standing-only Leppings Lane end of the ground allocated to Liverpool fans. An exit gate was opened to prevent any possible problems outside the ground and when match-goers flooded through it led to horrendous overcrowding in an already packed section. A few escaped, but men, women and children – who'd gone for a nice day out to watch their favourite team play a game of football – were killed in the crush. Ninety-six people died, a number that's been ingrained in all our memories since, making it the highest death toll at any disaster in British sporting history. Another 766 people were injured, and many of them never went to a match ever again.

Up in the press box that day, England World Cup-winning captain Bobby Moore was in tears as he dictated his comments for the next day's *Sunday Sport*. 'I left Hillsborough a broken man,' said his report. 'It doesn't matter who wins the cup now. It's tainted. I'm shattered. God help football. God bless those who died.'

The semi-final had been abandoned but when it was restaged at Old Trafford three weeks later Liverpool got through and went on to win the final at Wembley as well. In that match they beat close neighbours Everton 3-2 and fans of the rival clubs memorably and movingly combined in chants of 'Merseyside' to show their solidarity in desperately sad times.

An inquiry overseen by Lord Justice Taylor reported on the causes of the tragedy – and recommendations for safety at future sporting events included getting rid of standing terraces in favour of all-seater stadiums. The families and friends of those who lost their lives at Hillsborough in 1989 have had to live and cope with it every day since. But, amazingly, the legal consequences have still been proceeding more than 30 years later. Books and documentaries have been made about the disaster as loved ones bravely continue campaigns for legitimate final closure.

Devastatingly, Hillsborough wasn't the first time fans had died while enjoying the innocent pleasure of a Saturday afternoon out at a football match.

In Scotland, Ibrox Stadium in Glasgow has been the scene of two such tragedies. In 1902, part of a wooden terrace broke during a Scotland v England international and 26 people were killed. There was another awful calamity there in 1971 when a fan fell while leaving the stadium at the end of a Rangers match. Spectators rushing to leave ended up falling over each other down a long stairway and the death toll reached 66.

Months after the Second World War ended, what was the worst stadium tragedy at the time occurred at Bolton Wanderers in a match against Stoke. Crowds were huge as people tried to put the desolation of the war years firmly behind them, and the stadium was believed to be hugely over capacity. Metal crash barriers broke and 33 people were killed in the crush. A plaque commemorating the fans who died was unveiled by the late Nat Lofthouse in the Asda store which now stands on the site of the old Burnden Park ground.

It was little short of a riot at Luton in March 1985 during and after an FA Cup tie with Millwall, and one of the worst incidents of football hooliganism on record. Trouble began in the town with windows broken in shops and pubs as police struggled to cope. Inside the ground, Millwall fans invaded the pitch and hurled bottles, cans, nails and coins at home supporters fleeing up the terraces at the other end. The arrival of police dogs helped clear the pitch and the match started on time, although isolated fights were breaking out in the main stand. Luton won 1-0 and the players sprinted for safety as another pitch invasion took place, with seats torn out and used as weapons. A policeman was hit on the head in the centre circle by a concrete block and stopped breathing, but a colleague resuscitated him despite being punched and kicked himself. The carnage continued in the town afterwards with cars and windows smashed, and fights between fans and police. Altogether 81 people were injured, 31 of them police officers.

The tragedies continued and 56 people died and more than 250 suffered burns when a wooden stand caught fire at Bradford's Valley Parade ground a couple of months after the shame of the Luton-Millwall clashes. It was assumed a discarded cigarette had sparked a blaze in rubbish under the structure of the stand. Horrifically, the fire took just minutes to rage completely out of control and with the gates to the ground locked, the only escape for trapped fans was on to the pitch itself. Some, tragically, didn't even make that.

Incredible as it seems looking back now, the very same day fans died in the fire at Bradford, a 15-year-old boy was killed while going to his first football match. It was between Birmingham City and Leeds and there was trouble before the game and fighting in the ground, something almost to be expected at the time. The teenage lad was in the away end and died of head injuries after a wall collapsed and several fans were caught under it. A plaque commemorating him was later unveiled at St Andrew's with the inscription, 'As a football supporter, one of us, never to be forgotten.' Justice Oliver Popplewell, in a later report on sport's myriad problems, said it was more like the Battle of Agincourt than a football match that day.

Those issues of 1984/85 had been building up for months, with hooliganism and violence advancing more or less unchecked. Nobody seemed to know quite how to tackle it.

Southampton manager Lawrie McMenemy warned with prescience early that season, 'If nothing is done someone will get killed and it will finish football.' That was after his club banned Chelsea fans from football at The Dell for behaviour which terrorised people. At the same time, Leeds manager Eddie Gray decided his wife and family would no longer travel to away games following crowd violence at Huddersfield. 'The troublemakers are a disgrace and disgust me,' he said. Burton Albion were given a behind-closed-doors replay in the FA Cup against Leicester after a block of wood was thrown and knocked out their goalkeeper, while broken glass was scattered on the pitch at Coventry, where the club had previously been fined for a pitch invasion.

Although hooliganism was known abroad as 'the English disease', foreign clubs weren't immune from some horrible stuff. Inter Milan claimed a player was struck by something thrown from the crowd in their UEFA Cup semi-final with Real Madrid that season – but an appeal for a replay was turned down.

Chelsea chairman Ken Bates offered to concede his club's Milk Cup semi-final after supporters invaded the pitch when Sunderland scored, and mounted police had to be used to try and restore order. He said, 'There is an element of scum at most clubs and this particular scum must be driven out of their seats and back on the terraces where they can be adequately monitored.' Bates later announced plans to install an electric fence to deter pitch invaders but that idea was quickly shouted down. FA secretary Ted Croker pointed out that if such a fence had been in use at Bradford when the fire broke out, thousands more would have died as they would have been unable to escape on to the pitch.

Unbelievably, only a couple of weeks after the Bradford fire horror, 39 more fans died in the Heysel Stadium in

Brussels, chosen as the neutral venue for the European Cup Final between Liverpool and Juventus. The Belgian ground was a controversial selection for hosting the game and both clubs had unsuccessfully requested the match be staged elsewhere. It was an ageing arena with poor security and when Arsenal had played there the previous season they'd complained it wasn't fit for purpose.

There were rumours before the game that trouble was brewing following apparent attacks on Liverpool fans by supporters of AS Roma at the previous year's European Cup Final. An hour before the start, it began to kick off between the two sets of fans. Goading was followed by missile-throwing, and a fence separating the rival fans was broken. Italian fans trying to flee what seemed like an inevitable battle were crushed against a concrete wall which eventually collapsed. With police still battling to prevent Juventus fans from storming across the pitch to confront the Liverpool end, the match bizarrely went ahead. Juventus won 1-0 even though Liverpool players had said the last thing they wanted to do in the circumstances was play a game of football.

An official investigation was never ordered by UEFA. Eventually a Belgian judge investigated the circumstances of that night and concluded that Liverpool fans were to blame, but responsibility should also be shared by the football authorities for dismissing fears over Heysel's suitability as the host of a major final, and the police for failing to provide adequate crowd control. Fourteen Liverpool fans were found guilty of manslaughter.

English football was hammered by UEFA. Liverpool were banned from European competition for the next six years and there was a five-year blanket ban on all English clubs. Italy's national team manager Enzo Bearzot bravely adopted a different viewpoint, arguing that the only way to eradicate the problem was to ban hooligans, not clubs. And that, he pointed out, was a job for governments.

Prime Minister Margaret Thatcher never exactly came across as a fan of football but her government appreciated the need for action and produced a ten-point plan to combat hooliganism and ban alcohol from football grounds. A report was commissioned on both hooliganism and sports ground safety and recommendations included travel bans on away fans, membership cards, more closed-circuit TV surveillance, increased powers for the police, chanting of racial abuse to be a criminal offence, smoking to be banned in fire-risk stands, exits to be continually manned, and stewards to be trained in fire-fighting.

Hooliganism wasn't confined just to those times as violence had been associated with football for centuries, right back to when games were played in medieval times to settle disputes. Drink was often taken, serious injury or even death occurred, and games that had been arranged were often forbidden because of the dangers associated with them. Into the 20th century there were occasional fights and damage caused by vandals on their way back, usually, from days out at an away match.

Firms, as they were called, associated themselves with many clubs from the 1970s onwards and became notorious for their criminal behaviour. A fan was stabbed to death at Bolton, and fighting on and off the pitch at matches was commonplace. But tougher prison sentences began to be handed out and gradually the situation improved. Of the recommendations made by Justice Popplewell in his report, closed-circuit TV made a huge difference in making football grounds safer, and it's thought many of the hooligans drifted away to organised crime and left football to return to a more peaceful existence.

Just over a year after the horrors of Hillsborough, the country was enjoying the rejuvenating effects of Italia '90. That year's World Cup was a cracker. Paul Gascoigne cried, England played well and were plucky losers, and football edged its gradual way back towards nationwide affection.

Tony Williams, the editor of the *Barclays League Club Directory*, was able to write in the 1992 edition, 'Last season started in good spirit and, in general, football grounds became happier places. The young element of regular fans felt it was the in thing to be happy, have a laugh and even be friendly to the opposition. Old-fashioned standards were returning and football supporters enjoyed the new relaxing and enjoyable atmosphere.'

But having said that, finally in this chapter of depressing stories, the other major subject that has besmirched football is racism.

Don't suppose this was the first time it had happened in football but it's said that Dixie Dean was racially abused as he left the pitch at half-time in an Everton away match in 1930. Dean, who two years previously had set what must be an unbreakable record of scoring 60 goals in a First Division season, took one look at the abuser and punched him. No action was taken against the legendary Dean and a policeman who witnessed the incident is said to have told the victim he deserved it. That's how things used to be.

By the 1970s and '80s, racism had become rife in football with players abused by fans, offensive chanting on the terraces, and bananas thrown on to pitches.

During that time, Viv Anderson became the first black player to represent England, but that didn't make him immune from racism. He told the *Nottingham Post*, 'I'd just got into the Nottingham Forest team and the abuse I got at an away game as I walked out before the game was so severe I had to go back into the dressing room. I told the manager, Brian Clough, I didn't think I could play. He told me not to go down that route and I was playing. There was no escape, I had to cope with it.'

Tough love from Clough, and other players like John Barnes, Clyde Best, Garth Crooks and Cyrille Regis all suffered unforgivable abuse and had to ignore it – Barnes was pictured scornfully back-heeling a banana off a pitch at one match. Fair play to Barcelona defender Dani Alves who picked up a banana thrown on to the field in Spain, peeled it, and took a bite out of it. Brazil international Alves was taking a corner in a match in 2014 and the Villarreal fan who threw it was identified and banned for life.

Former Jamaica international Jason Euell has clear memories of suffering racial abuse while he was on the substitutes' bench for Blackpool at Stoke in 2009. Euell told Henry Winter much later in an interview with *The Times*, 'Fair play to Stoke, they dealt with it and the fan was thrown out and received a three-year banning order. I was more frustrated in the people around him than I was with the person who actually said it. It was all of a sudden, look forward, blinkers on, earplugs in. "Didn't hear anything, he's not even a regular fan." That's irrelevant. You've allowed it to happen, you haven't spoken up.'

Jason's words really registered with me as I was on the terraces at a non-league match in Oxfordshire sometime in the 1990s when a player was racially abused. I turned round and called the man out, saying what he'd shouted was totally out of order. I'm not boasting about it, but I was with my teenage son and I wanted him to recognise that such abuse was abhorrent. Not that he didn't know it full well by that age. The fan in question backed down when I confronted him, mumbling, 'Well, he's shit anyway.' I agreed with him that may well have been the case, but that didn't justify what he'd said. And then we carried on watching the match as if nothing had happened. I'd never thought of that incident in terms of Jason's words about how frustrated he was that everyone else around us didn't weigh in.

While our stadiums are thankfully 100 times safer now, and hooliganism has seemingly dwindled to virtually nothing, racist, anti-semitic and homophobic abuse has continued in football in this country into the 21st century. Whenever you suspect it might be gradually waning – in football, if not society – then something ugly rears its head again. One step forward, one step back. We didn't take enough notice of Harry Redknapp, when managing Spurs, who said succinctly, 'Anyone who does it should be put in prison – not banned from football. Stick them where they belong, in the nut-house.'

There was vile racist abuse of England players in away internationals, and of Raheem Sterling in a match at Chelsea. At least that supporter was identified and given a lifetime ban, while five other fans at that match were excluded for one- or two-year periods. In Italy, Belgium international Romelu Lukaku had monkey chants aimed at him as he took a penalty for Inter Milan and said afterwards he felt the game was heading backwards. England international Jadon Sancho said incidents of racism made him question why he played football and that he feared such abuse could make players lose their love of the sport. Former Manchester City midfielder Yaya Touré was quoted as saying he believed racism in football was getting worse because 'fans are more stupid than before'.

Then there was sporadic booing of taking the knee at matches, and vile online racist abuse of players when followers hid behind anonymity to call them out for so-called mistakes in games. Even Marcus Rashford, surely the man of 2020 for his marvellous contributions and interventions in the year of coronavirus, was targeted. Once more there was a lot of talk about how to solve it, and how to catch the culprits, but no real solutions. At least one referee, as well as a female TV pundit, were also subjected to shocking abuse. The perpetrators are such a tiny majority among tens of millions who would never dream of doing such a thing, but that of course doesn't heal the wounds or solve the problem.

There's also been a continuing deep-rooted problem at grassroots level. At Sporting Bengal, formed in 1996 to encourage Asian football in London, the players and

FOOTBALL IS BETTER WITH FANS

coaching staff have always experienced discrimination. Coach Imrul Gazi told a BBC investigation, 'The biggest problem is parents on the sidelines. They're the worst culprits in youth football.'

The Kick It Out organisation, which promotes equality in football, said some people have been racially abused for so long they've become numb to it and don't report it because they feel there's no effective method of support.

Ex-England player Viv Anderson added, 'At least in my day you could look the person in the face who was abusing you. Now they're just hiding under different accounts, on different social media platforms. I think it's a lot more difficult for players now. The abuse used to be confined to the stadium, and once I left the pitch it finished. For today's players there is no getting away from it.'

In *The Times* in February 2021, James Gheerbrant linked the outbreak of deeply offensive online abuse with fans not being able to go to matches. He wrote, 'Covid has robbed us of the physical proximity of being in the stadium. In this yawning chasm, the toxic forces of hate and cyber rage thrive.' I'm not sure that I agree with this conclusion, beyond the simple explanation that a lot of probably sad and lonely keyboard warriors were left with too much time on their hands. As Gheerbrant pointed out, 'The roots of football's rage problem run deep and can't be solved without solving such embedded issues as racial prejudice, toxic masculinity and the shift that social media has precipitated in our public discourse.'

11

Charities: Marching on together

AND NOW for the good news. After a miserable chapter dealing with football's distasteful side, we wash our hands and bounce back with some of the huge charity efforts the beautiful sport has contributed to making the world a better place.

Clubs, managers, players and supporters have all played their part over the years in helping their communities, but even more so during the pandemic. As stated previously, England international Marcus Rashford played a stunningly impressive part in using his softly spoken but powerful voice to persuade the government to do more to help under-privileged children. He was an inspiration, and fans queued up to donate to the FairShare charity he was backing.

Many Manchester United fans were so moved that they donated all their money received in refunds from the club when supporters were shut out of games due to coronavirus, and promised that the rest of any refunds would be handed over as well.

Exactly one year after the start of the first lockdown, the millionth food parcel was supplied through an initiative by the English Football League. Nottingham Forest's Ryan Yates delivered that particular selection as part of EFL's community work. All 72 clubs took part in helping deliver food, PPE and prescriptions, as well as making more than half a million calls to fans and vulnerable people, and allowing stadiums to be used for vaccination and testing by the NHS.

One of the first clubs to take action to support their local elderly and vulnerable were Stevenage where chairman Phil Wallace thanked fans for immediately getting involved and said such wartime spirit was what the club was all about. They also came up with a lovely visual aid, advertising their next match on the big fixture board outside the ground as Stevenage v Coronavirus.

Following a torrid relationship between fans and their club for a while, Blackpool have been busily rebuilding bridges and the supporters' trust raised £25,000 to ensure children from poorer local families got a Christmas present during lockdown. And new owner Simon Sadler matched it with £25,000 of his own money.

Rashford and international team-mate Jordan Henderson were by no means the only footballers to help good causes, while fans also gave thousands to charity when they boycotted televised games featuring the clubs they supported, in protest at TV companies imposing pay-per-view restrictions. Liverpool's Spirit of Shankly group set themselves a target to raise £10,000 from fans refusing to pay fees – and they actually collected more than ten times that for foodbank charities. Supporters of, among others, Arsenal, Newcastle, Manchester United, Wolves, Aston Villa, Spurs and Leeds all joined the pay-per-view protest and raised cash for charity.

It's hardly surprising that someone who'd just won an award from the Football Supporters' Association should praise fans at this time. But Henry Winter of *The Times*, who was chosen as Writer of the Year at the FSA awards in March 2021, was genuine when he praised football's lockdown heroes who had got stuck in by delivering food parcels, raising funds for their communities, and phoning isolated people. And he praised the many fans who rebelled over pay-per-view. 'What the fans did there was incredibly important,' he said. 'If anyone questioned the importance of fans, they won't now – games are soulless and soundless without fans. I hope that after this pandemic fans get the treatment and respect they deserve.'

Meanwhile, in this chapter of good people, Burnley fan Scott Cunliffe completed an incredible charity effort during the 2018/19 Premier League season when he ran to every one of his team's away games. The marathon meant him covering more than 3,000 miles and he's believed to be the first man ever to complete that particular challenge. The fixture list did Scott no favours as Burnley had three away matches in London over 22 days in December, and his commitment was to start each away trip from Burnley's Turf Moor ground. So he ended up running every day for a fortnight, either on the way to London or back again, in a successful bid to get to all the matches on time. Scott had previously spent 20 years working for charities in

Indonesia and East Timor and violent wars and poverty-hit environments left him with depression and post-traumatic stress disorder. Running played a huge part in his recovery and he was keen to use his love of ultra marathons to positive effect. He raised £60,000 for the club's official charity, Burnley FC in the Community, which helps initiatives in the town and also all over the country.

There must be something in the air around Burnley – good people doing amazing things. Following Scott's amazing running contribution, a Clarets supporter decided to run two kilometres every day for 50 days to raise money for Royal Manchester Children's Hospital. And the runner, Freddie Xavi, was only nine years old. He completed the 50-day challenge on Christmas Day 2020 and even put off opening his presents that day because of his commitment to the cause. Freddie took up the challenge to boost the spirits of his best mate, Hughie Higginson, who had been diagnosed with acute lymphoblastic leukaemia. He aimed to raise £1,000 but massive publicity helped swell the fund to more than 100 times that. His proud mum said Freddie was a kind and thoughtful boy, while Hughie's mother didn't hold back, saying he was an amazing little star. And one viewer of a BBC report of the event commented, 'Everyone should have a friend like Freddie!'

Elsewhere, football fans did a brilliant volunteering job when they went to South Africa for the 2010 World Cup. You know, the vuvuzela one. They spent their days helping to build an orphanage for some of the country's most deprived children, and the evenings watching World Cup matches on TV or actually in the stadiums for England group matches. The new-build was in an area where 70 per cent of the population are infected by HIV or AIDS. It took the four friends from the Isle of Wight – Martin Boyce, Steve Goodall, Len Hill and Paul Martin – two and a half weeks to complete the building, along with other volunteers. Steve told the BBC, 'Getting up in the early hours, slogging all day, for guys not in the building trade, it was quite an experience.' Martin added, 'We worked hard and changed people's lives. We gave kids who have nothing somewhere to live where they'll be looked after and fed, and that's marvellous.'

The trip was organised by the Lionsraw charity which was set up by pastor and football fan Jon Burns to demonstrate the good that supporters can do. About 200 football fans went to South Africa under the scheme to take part in soccer schools and construction projects. Martin said, 'Everything was brilliant – apart from the football!'

Africa also benefitted from an initiative which fans of Everton, Southampton and Hull City took on board. They donated spare tops and shorts as part of a Kits For Africa campaign to help support grassroots football for the under-privileged.

A football-mad 11-year-old set her heart on completing a challenge to do 7.1 million keepy-uppies – but her parents worked out it would take her 97 years to complete at her rate of 200 a day! So Imogen Papworth-Heidel, an Arsenal fan who lives in Cambridgeshire, upped her commitment to 7,000 a day during the 2020 lockdown and school summer holidays. And the family also hit on the bright idea of asking others to donate, and 2,000 people sent in videos of themselves keeping-uppy. While Imogen managed more than a million herself, all the other donated ones took it over the 7.1 million target. And why that number? Because it was one for every key worker in the UK at the time. She raised more than £10,000 to be shared between nine worthy charities. Her proud dad said, 'She could easily have sat with her Xbox or played computer games but actually what she did was go out into the garden, rain or shine, and just bang them out.'

A fan who missed playing for his local team during lockdown set himself a challenge of running ten kilometres a day for a week to keep fit. Liam Noble decided to turn it into a charity effort and aimed to raise £200 for mental health charity Mind. But the support kept growing and growing and Bristol Rovers fan Liam, who's had a season ticket since he was three, ended up donating £3,500. He said, 'I don't run too much and it was a big challenge. I had great support from Rovers fans who kept texting me saying "you've got this".' Bristol Rovers manager Paul Tisdale called it a fantastic effort and said, 'Our players average about 11km in a match and 7km in training every day so he's done more than professional footballers.'

A stag do for 36 football fans 20 years ago has mushroomed into a charity group that has since raised £75,000 for good causes, including the Sir Bobby Robson Foundation, a cancer research charity. It all started with a trip to the horse racing at Chester by supporters from the Chester-le-Street area of Durham, and the group grew to around 200 members. Talking of Bobby Robson, he was a much-loved man who represented all that was good about football. He was well known for his quotes, and of the many when he was England manager I love the one about the 1990 World Cup match against Cameroon: 'We didn't underestimate them. They were just a lot better than we thought,' he replied.

Two schoolboy Liverpool fans from Surrey decided in lockdown to raise money for their local hospital and hit on the idea of running and rowing the distance they live from Anfield. So Ben Tabberner (14) and his 11-year-old brother Henry ran either on local roads or on a treadmill at home, as well as using a home rowing machine to achieve their target of completing a distance of 322km.

Another young supporter, 12-year-old Newcastle fanatic Jamie Stuart, wrote a football magazine as part of a home-school project during lockdown. He sent it to family and friends in return for a donation to the Sir Bobby Robson Foundation, and raised hundreds of pounds. But even better than that, he got a lovely message in return from charity patron and Newcastle legend Alan Shearer. 'I know your dad is a big fan of Newcastle, as you are, so I just want to say thank you very much and well done,' said Big Al.

Football-loving Tabitha Ryan, also 12, completed 26,000 penalties and 26,000 keepy-uppies in her back garden in Merthyr during lockdown to raise money for sight loss charity RNIB Cymru, while Crystal Palace fan Paul Browning co-ordinated a fund raising online campaign which raised £16,000 for St John Ambulance. The money was presented to volunteers from the charity on the pitch at half-time of a game at Selhurst Park.

A 50-mile walk by fans raised thousands for charity, but more than that it was about teamwork, empathy and friendship. Thirty-nine-year-old Alex Broadley was a Fulham supporter who suffered from depression and sadly took his own life in June 2020. Fifteen of his friends and family, many of them followers of Brighton & Hove Albion, decided to walk from the Seagulls' ground to Fulham before the two clubs played each other later that year. They smashed their £5,000 target to raise money for Campaign Against Living Miserably and collected £18,000. They found it pretty tough in wind and rain, but got through it together. Also in Alex's memory, his brother Dan completed the same distance in sunshine in Australia wearing a Fulham shirt.

Even though one of them supports Manchester United and the other is a Liverpool fan, Scott Baron and Craig Hoyland are best mates who worked together to raise hundreds of pounds for charity. They spent 11 hours walking the 34 miles from Anfield to Old Trafford to benefit charities supporting war veterans and cancer victims.

Also stepping out were a group of Wolves fans who trekked from Wolverhampton to Birmingham to raise funds to help pay for specialist treatment for a young girl in need of life-changing treatment. When he heard about their long-distance effort, West Brom supporter Chris Jebb donated his Wolves football programme collection dating back to 1948 to be sold at a charity auction to boost the fund.

Good efforts by everyone, fair play to them.

And to end with, a lovely charitable gesture by a football club, rather than kind-hearted charity-minded individuals. After winning the Dutch League in 2021 for the 35th time, Ajax melted down the championship trophy they'd just been presented with. From it they made little commemorative stars to send to all 42,000 fans who had renewed their season tickets without being able to go to games because of coronavirus. Literally, the club had shared the trophy with their fans.

12

Social media: You only sing when you're winning

EVERY FAN'S a critic – in the nicest possible way, of course – and many clearly fancy that they could do a better job than the manager who's spent a lifetime in professional football and got all their coaching badges after retiring from a successful playing career.

Twitter gives supporters the ideal platform as it's easy to use, and whatever's said is just as easily forgotten in a matter of minutes. Fans can vent their spleen there, show how clever they are, or just say something funny that makes us all laugh. It would be great, sometimes, if they just stuck to the amusing ones and forgot about the others.

But before considering a few of those highly amusing, or provocative, tweets, it's possible that ringing radio station talk-ins to discuss your team's performance is probably a bit old-school now. But West Ham supporter Paul couldn't resist it after a win for his team in the 2020/21 season. He called talkSPORT to say every player was brilliant and it had been a super performance. So superb, Paul revealed movingly, that he'd actually cried. Then he added, 'I know we've only beaten Crystal Palace, but what a night!'

On the other hand, I saw a tweet from a Hammers follower who was blowing bubbles in fury after they'd just lost to reigning champions Liverpool, having won six on the bounce leading up to that game. You can't please everybody all the time. And staying with West Ham, fan Lloyd Austin shared with us all his dad's Boxing Day message to him: 'Hello Lloyd, hope you had a good Christmas. Why is Noble playing?' James was taking it all in his stride: 'As a Hammers fan of many years' standing, trying to predict anything they do is nigh on impossible – in a weird sort of way that is part of the attraction.'

Mark in Stockport tweeted, 'Manchester City are a very exciting team but sometimes they can be very boring to watch with their Chuckle Brothers brand of to-you, to-me, to-you type football.'

Francis Edwards commented about Chelsea that they 'play like a group of good players who meet on a Sunday for a game', while Stuart said that one of their players 'would be too pedestrian for my uncle's walking football team'.

Jake let everyone know his views on Manchester United: 'The emotional rollercoaster that happens every game may not be to some fans' liking, but that's the idea of the sport. I haven't shouted so much at my telly in years.'

Noel Fitzpatrick: 'This "it was on his weaker foot" drives me crazy! These guys are professional footballers! They spend all week kicking a ball. They should be just as good on either foot, they're not centipedes!'

Anonymous: 'I met the great Bobby Robson at Italia '90, lovely man, always had the time for a nice chat. And then Gazza nudged in and said, "Doing any shagging, lads?"'

Jon: 'The range of responses to that red card underlines the absolute impossible job that refs are expected to do. The sense of entitlement among football fans is very particular to the sport.'

Vaass: 'It annoys me when the more successful teams take digs at the less successful ones. Smaller teams actually take care of their fans while bigger clubs just see them as a customer.'

Dean: 'Who would be in your top five players of all time? I would go with Pelé, Maradona, George Best, Cristiano Ronaldo, Lionel Messi and Patrick Bamford.' (Actually, I make that six!)

TV presenter Richard Osman: 'I wonder if I'll ever get to an age when I realise nothing I do will affect the result of the match I'm watching.'

Match of the Day host Gary Lineker: 'Pundits upset football clubs from time to time. Pundits upset football fans from time to time. Football clubs and their fans are very sensitive and extremely tribal. It's part of the pundit's job to give opinions and it's a sign of their effectiveness when clubs and fans pile on.'

Stephen: 'Give me getting hammered at home by Wigan in the Third Division in front of 2k real fans over the Prem any day of the week.'

Terry Pratchett: 'The thing about football – the important thing about football – is that it's not just about football.' (I'm still working that one out, but I'm sure it's profound).

Gary: 'Entertainment is fine, but winning is better.' (That reminded me of something Lou Macari was quoted as saying when he was manager of Birmingham: 'When people tell me that fans want entertainment and style first I don't believe it. Fans want to win. Style's a bonus.')

Brendan: 'Men are generally brought up to contain their emotions, therefore sport, and football in particular, are a valve to release pent-up frustration and indeed love.'

Anonymous: 'Good players practise until they get it right. But great players practise until they never get it wrong.'

Journalist Henry Winter: 'VAR has some important elements, namely catching howlers, but this micro-refereeing of matches rips the joy from games. Football belongs to players and supporters not [David] Elleray and [Mike] Riley.' Carl commented: 'VAR – football managed perfectly well without it for over 100 years. Scrap it. The End.'

Sam: 'As a Newcastle United fan I would sever and eat my own arm to have José [Mourinho] at my club.' Talk about an armless threat.

Tom: 'The boy Rashford should really have a couple of goals to his name. It's nothing to do with his contribution, it's just that he's such a smashing young man I want to see him doing well.'

Dale Humphries: 'Any parents struggling to get the little ones to sleep? Put this match on and stick them in front of the telly!'

Tattz: 'Speaking as a neutral, this game is a shadow of what it used to be. No two-footed lunges, no naughty off-the-ball antics, no squaring up of the managers on the touchline. Where is the passion? This feels dry.'

Gary R: 'I remember as a kid watching games and thinking "nobody deserves to lose this". These days I watch them and think "nobody deserves to win this".'

Sophie Gayter: 'I fear games like this will be more commonplace as the season goes on. Both teams sloppy, fatigued spent forces. Genuinely feel a bit sorry for these guys having to play and deliver entertaining football every three days.'

Anonymous: 'My partner just split up with me because she thinks I'm obsessed with football. I'm a bit gutted about it – we've been going out for three seasons.'

I think that's a good time to leave Twitter to its own amusement. But still on the subject of 'new' media, it was Sir Winston Churchill who said, 'A pessimist sees the difficulty in every opportunity; an optimist sees the opportunity in every difficulty.' Well, the coronavirus pandemic was assuredly a 'difficulty' but optimistic and predominantly young football fans jumped at the chance to establish new ways for us to follow our favourite clubs. Fan TV channels provided live commentaries on games, as well as match previews, player ratings, and interviews with players and managers, and they soared in popularity.

One of Liverpool's most popular fan channels, TheRedmenTV, has nearly half a million followers – including the club's manager, Jürgen Klopp. One of five people who works full-time on the channel, Ross Chandley, told the BBC, 'Even before the lockdown there were a lot of people who couldn't go to Anfield. We have a big following across the world because we provide context and culture to people who are in love with the club. I went to the Club World Cup in Qatar when Liverpool were there and someone shouted over to me, "Oh Redmen TV." It was a guy from Syria, a war-torn country, and he's getting something from our content to feel more like a Liverpool fan. It blew my mind.

'Some people may not have anyone else to talk to, they might not have a group of friends where they are who are into the club. But we provide somewhere they can go, a place with people they can chat to.'

A pioneer of fan channels, Mark Goldbridge set up The United Stand as he was keen to share his post-match thoughts with fellow Manchester United supporters. But it's now a major undertaking. 'I started a show on a Sunday night with a few others where we'd chat and there were about ten people watching. But it kept growing and they kept asking us to do the games live.' Its success has enabled him to turn a passion into a career which is now a fast-growing industry.

Before social media, what on earth did we do with our time? Well, watched television for one. So what do the names Jack Halford, Gerry Standing and Brian Lane mean to you? Telly addicts might recognise them as the original detectives in the popular long-running series *New Tricks*. Whereas West Bromwich fans will also know that Halford Standing Lane just happens to be the oldest stand at The Hawthorns. The show's co-creator, Roy Mitchell, is a big Baggies fan and took great pleasure in naming characters in the series after players from his favourite club.

I'm sure Roy wasn't the first TV writer to pay tribute to his club in this way. There was once an episode of police drama series *Dixon of Dock Green* that featured all characters with the surnames of Spurs players. The writer, Ted Willis, was born locally and now rests in peace in Tottenham Cemetery.

The 1971 thriller *Get Carter*, starring Michael Caine, had a crime boss called Cyril Kinnear – Spurs' well-known full-backs at the time were Joe Kinnear and Cyril Knowles, so it would be amazing if that was just a coincidence. More bizarrely, three of the thugs in the 2001 film *Antitrust* were called Redmond Schmeichel, Danny Solskjaer and Randy Sheringham. Mischievous or not?

And Rodney Trotter in the much-loved *Only Fools and Horses* had the middle name Charlton after his south London roots, though he'll always be Dave to his mate Trigger. Or Plonker to his brother.

13

Fan power: We'll keep on fighting until the end

MANY FOOTBALL fans reckon their most important job is to intimidate the opposition. They can't have any direct effect on what's happening on the pitch, where it matters most, but they can offer insults, barracking and abuse from the safety of the sidelines. I'm not quite sure if any footballer has ever been 'mentally disintegrated', as they call it in cricket when sledging is reckoned to have been successful, but it's always worth a try.

The most memorable example of attempted intimidation – with explosive results – happened at Selhurst Park on 25 January 1995. In a no-love-lost encounter between Crystal Palace and champions Manchester United, tackles were flying in and tempers fraying. Suddenly it all got too much for United talisman Eric Cantona and he retaliated by kicking out at home defender Richard Shaw. The Frenchman was sent off by the referee – but the red mist hadn't lifted even as he reluctantly trudged away towards the tunnel.

Suddenly, Cantona dramatically reacted to comments by a Palace fan who had made his way down to the front of the stand. In a never-to-be-forgotten moment the United player launched an extraordinary flying kung-fu kick into the chest of the supporter. He was dragged away before further blows could be struck, and escorted to the dressing room, but TV cameras had captured the incident in all its amazing detail.

To be repeated another 93 times on TV the next day – at least that was the complaint from United manager Sir Alex Ferguson. In all honesty, though, that was hardly a surprise given the fact that nothing quite like it had ever happened before or since.

The Palace fan was reported in *The Sun* as having admitted he might have sworn, but said that Cantona was the lunatic, not him. Former United head of security 'Ned' Kelly remembered in an interview with the BBC years later, 'This chap just came straight down the gangway and started screaming abuse at Eric. He was okay when the guy was effing and jeffing at him but I think he called his mother a "French whore" and that was the turning point. The next thing I know Eric is over the barrier giving him a kung-fu kick.'

Cantona's colleague David Beckham was 19 at the time and was in the stand that night. He said in his book, *My Side*, 'I think it was just an instinctive reaction, a natural thing to do. Anybody getting that sort of abuse in the street would have reacted in the same way. Just because Eric was a professional footballer, in the spotlight, didn't stop him behaving like anyone else might have done.'

United suspended and fined Cantona, and the FA extended the ban so he was out of football for several months. He also had to appear at East Croydon magistrates court where he admitted assault and was given 120 hours' community service. He returned to football during the following season and helped Manchester United to a league and cup double, but retired in the summer of 1997. The fan also appeared in court and was fined with threatening behaviour.

Cantona was a complex and controversial character. Far from being sorry about what happened that night at Selhurst Park, he said 25 years later for a new film, *The United Way*, 'I have one regret. I would have loved to have kicked him even harder!' Whether it was before or after he kung-fu kicked one of them I'm not sure, but Cantona apparently said once, 'English fans are brilliant. In England when you ask someone which club he supports, it means something. The guy supports a club for the whole of his life, whatever the ups and downs. In France, there's no loyalty. If you're not top of the league, the fans go to another club.'

Fancy flying into a foreign airport for a European fixture to be greeted by the intimidating sign 'Welcome to Hell'. That's what happened to Manchester United in 1993 when they touched down in Istanbul to play the notoriously inhospitable Galatasaray. Turkish fans had been let in to the airport to threaten United with warnings that it would be their last 48 hours alive. At their hotel before the game, cash went missing from the players' rooms and they were woken continuously through the night by rogue phone calls. The police helped out, too, arresting more than 150

United fans and chucking them into cells so they would miss the game. Welcome to Hell, indeed. It was before another match involving Galatasaray, in April 2000, when two Leeds fans were killed. Chris Loftus and Kevin Speight were stabbed on the eve of a UEFA Cup semi-final and after a lengthy legal process, four men were jailed for their part in the murders.

Perhaps a subsequent 5-0 defeat by Celtic was more significant, but a demonstration by hoodied Rangers fans almost certainly played some part in the appointment of Liverpool legend Steven Gerrard as the club's new manager in 2018. Exasperated at Rangers' performances at the time, and probably even more hurt by Celtic's domination of Old Firm games, a group of fans took matters into their own hands. Overnight, they padlocked the gates to the Rangers training round and left behind a home-made banner saying, 'We deserve better.' Within weeks, Gerrard had been appointed and the charismatic ex-England international gradually transformed the club and restored the faith of devoted supporters, so much so he led Rangers to the Scottish Premiership title in his third season.

It's no fun being a goalkeeper in front of a hostile crowd. Warming up for the second leg of the 1967 Intercontinental Cup Final in Buenos Aires against Racing Club of Argentina, Celtic's Scotland international goalkeeper Ronnie Simpson was hit by a missile believed to be fired from a catapult in the crowd. He was dazed enough to have to go off and miss the match. Celtic feared that staging a walkout in protest might make the atmosphere even worse and fulfilled the fixture, though they lost 1-0.

Fan for life: The picture that sums up the joy of football as Newcastle United supporters enjoy a 2014 victory over Manchester City in the League Cup. (Photo: Lindsey Parnaby/AFP via Getty Images)

Flare-up: Arsenal fans protest outside the Emirates Stadium in April 2021 against the club's owners just after the proposal to join the European Super League was dropped. (Photo: Chloe Knott – Danehouse/Getty Images)

Ill-timed: Atletico Madrid supporters out in force at Liverpool for a Champions League game in March 2020 just before the country went into lockdown because of coronavirus. (Photo: Javier Soriano – AFP via Getty Images)

Easy does it: Just 2,000 Manchester City fans were allowed into Wembley to see their team win the Carabao Cup Final in April 2021 as football edged its way back after the pandemic. (Photo: Matt McNulty – Manchester City/Manchester City FC via Getty Images)

Happy days: Spurs fans celebrate an Eric Dier goal in their Premier League local derby with West Ham in August 2014. (Photo: Jamie McDonald/ Getty Images)

Passion: Shrewsbury Town fans let their hair down to celebrate victory at Charlton in a Sky Bet League One semi-final play-off in 2018 – but they lost the final to Rotherham. (Picture: Ian Scammell)

Spot the rock star: Wolves fan and Led Zeppelin lead singer Robert Plant among supporters at Molineux in 2018 celebrating the club's promotion to the Premier League. (Photo: Sam Bagnall – AMA/ Getty Images)

Devoted: Portsmouth fan John Westwood – in the words of his portrait painter 'externalising his deep passion for Portsmouth FC as well as reflecting his inner self.' (Photo: Sam Bagnall/AMA/Corbis via Getty Images)

Celebrity fans: Lifelong West Bromwich Albion supporters Adrian Chiles and Frank Skinner together at The Hawthorns for the 2019 visit of Blackburn. (Photo: Adam Fradgley – AMA/WBA FC via Getty Images)

Some you win: Brighton fans wear masks depicting deputy prime minister John Prescott in 2004 as they successfully campaign for his permission to build a new stadium for their club who were homeless at the time. (Photo: Christopher Lee/ Getty Images)

Rock on: Great day out for thousands of Blackpool fans as an open top bus takes players and their families along the promenade after winning promotion to the Premier League in 2010. (Photo: Andrew Yates/AFP via Getty Images)

Altogether now: Singer-songwriter Jamie Webster entertains Liverpool fans before a friendly against Borussia Dortmund in the USA in July 2019. (Photo: John Powell/Liverpool FC via Getty Images)

Flashpoint: Angry Eric Cantona is taunted by the Crystal Palace crowd after being sent off while playing for Manchester United at Selhurst Park in 1995. (Photo: Shaun Botterill/Allsport)

Marathon effort: Burnley fan Scott Cunliffe chalks up another ground on his successful challenge of running to all his team's away games during the 2018/19 season. This time he's greeted on arrival at Watford. (Photo: Richard Heathcote/ Getty Images)

Tradition: Win, lose or draw, non-league players thank their fans in person for their support. This time, it's Sittingbourne players at the end of an Isthmian League match at Hastings. (Photo: Ken Medwyn)

Life and limb: Millwall fans take a huge risk by climbing a floodlight pylon to get a panoramic view of their team's FA Cup win over Newcastle in January 1957. (Photo: Keystone-France/ Gamma-Keystone via Getty Images)

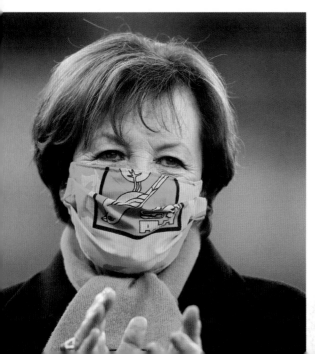

Masked-up: Norwich City director Delia Smith welcomes fans in December 2020 when a limited number were allowed back for what turned out to be a very brief time. (Photo: Stephen Pond/Getty Images)

The old supporters' chant of 'what's it like to see a crowd' would have had special meaning for another international goalkeeper, Dick Pym. He was 'between the sticks', as they used to call it, for Bolton Wanderers in the 1923 FA Cup Final, the first to be played at Wembley. It's thought that twice as many people as the official limit of 125,000 squeezed into the newly built stadium that day. Kick-off was delayed by 40 minutes as the police, famously led by an officer on a white horse, gradually pushed the crowd back off the pitch. But the game was played with the crowd just inches behind the touchline, and the nets in the goal torn to shreds. Dick, in goal, could not only 'see a crowd' but he could touch them if he stretched out his arms, and would have been able to feel their breath on his neck.

Bolton won 2-0 and Pym went on to establish a record as the only goalkeeper to play in three cup finals and not concede a goal. He also played international football and lived to the grand old age of 95, setting another record of being the longest-lived England player. He gave an interview to Raymond Maule for a Blackpool matchday programme when he was well into his 80s and was critical of the violence and hooliganism that had latched itself on to football. He said, 'Back in my playing days we used to get a bit of kidding from the crowd, but that was all.'

It just shows how careful you have to be when advertising a friendly and talking about the star players who are going to turn out for the opposition. The mighty Cristiano Ronaldo featured heavily in the pre-match advertisements when his club Juventus were about to play a 2019 friendly in South Korea. But Ronaldo failed to make it off the bench, and some of the 65,000 fans at the match successfully sued for 'emotional distress' and got their money back. Plus compensation!

A year earlier, Ronaldo scored one of football's greatest ever goals, a brilliant overhead bicycle kick while he was at least two metres up in the air. It helped his Real Madrid team beat Juventus in the Champions League in 2018. Home fans generously applauded Ronaldo for his strike, which Juventus defender Andrea Barzagli memorably described as a 'PlayStation goal'. The great man himself was stunned by the reaction of the Italian fans. Ronaldo said, 'I have to say thank you to all the supporters of Juventus. What they did for me was amazing. This has never happened in my career so far.' And a couple of months later, at the end of that season, who did did Ronaldo join when he left Real Madrid? Well, Juventus. Coincidence or not?

When Cologne qualified for European football for the first time in 25 years, their fans desperately wanted to see the big return. It was away to Arsenal in the Europa League in 2017, and the ticket allocation for the German club was 2,900. But an estimated 20,000 fans travelled over hoping they'd be let into the stadium anyway. Some of them got tickets directly from Arsenal fans, ranging from gifts to pretty high mark-ups, and Cologne were fined £53,000 by UEFA for what happened that night.

The Guardian took a magnificent photograph at the Euro 2016 group stage match between England and Wales. It shows an England fan in a white replica team shirt watching the match in the middle of at least 60 red-shirted Welsh supporters. You can imagine from his face the concern when he realised his ticket had got him into the wrong end. But the great thing about the picture is that everyone seems intent on watching the game and ignoring the guy who sticks out like a sore thumb. One day, hopefully, such a picture won't even be worth talking about.

Early in his football career, Vinnie Jones was playing for Wealdstone in the Conference – or the Gola League as it was in the early 1980s – and his team were leading 2-0 when a thick mist began to sweep over Frickley Athletic's Yorkshire ground. Home fans had the bright idea of lighting a fire behind the goal, and the heavy smoke blended in with the thickening fog to make visibility even worse. In his autobiography, *Vinnie*, the footballer-turned-filmstar recalled, 'The attempted sabotage had the opposite effect as the referee said, "Right, that's it, we're going to finish this match now at all costs."' And finish it they did, even though by the end the players in the penalty area couldn't see their colleague taking a corner. Vinnie's conclusion: 'It was the first time I ever shook a referee's hand and meant it.'

14

Players: He's one of our own

NO FAN has ever got closer to a player than Spurs supporter
Andrew Deaner. He was at White Hart Lane with his brothers
for an FA Cup tie against Bolton in March 2012 when one
of the visiting players, Fabrice Muamba, suddenly collapsed.
By day, Andrew is a consultant cardiologist in a London
hospital and he immediately realised the player had suffered
a cardiac arrest. He persuaded a steward to let him through
and he dashed on to the pitch to work with the clubs' medical
teams to keep Fabrice alive. After several defibrillator shocks,
Andrew went with Fabrice to hospital where he gradually
recovered. The midfielder's heart had stopped for 78 minutes
in all and he had to retire from playing the game he loved.
Cardiologist Andrew told the BBC about that night, 'If you
are ever going to use the term miraculous I suppose it could
be used here.' Eight months later, Muamba returned to White
Hart Lane and was given a standing ovation by the fans.

The eternally grateful Fabrice aside, what do the players
themselves really think of the fans? The legend that was

Jimmy Greaves had a few thoughts on the matter in his book, *My World of Soccer*, written in 1966. 'You cannot beat the company of the terrace boys,' he wrote. 'You will find some of the fairest-minded football critics in the world, and many are first-class comedians. Despite the fact the terrace fans are well conditioned against adverse weather, I feel they deserve the same protection as the man who pays a pound for his seat in the stands.'

I don't think I was either the critic or the comedian Greavsie was talking about, but I know that if I were to list the best players I've ever seen, the great man would be in my top three. It was about the time of his book being written that I remember a goal he scored at White Hart Lane for Spurs against Preston. Perhaps memory plays tricks but my recollection is that to get past the last defender and then the goalkeeper, Greaves didn't touch the ball once. A shimmy of his body one way and the defender was on the ground, the other way and down went the keeper. He just carried on and steered the ball into the empty net, and celebrated in a typical shrugging-shoulders modest Greaves sort of way in front of understandably delighted fans.

Apart from that, Georgi, how are you settling down in England with your new club? Macedonia international Georgi Hristov joined Barnsley for £1m in 1997 and managed to offend the whole Yorkshire town with an interview he gave to a sports magazine back in Belgrade. 'I'm finding it difficult to settle into a decent way of life,' he was reported as saying. 'The local girls are far uglier than the ones back in Macedonia. Our women are much prettier and besides, they don't drink as much beer as the Barnsley girls which is something I don't like at all. England is a strange country and I found it hard to adapt to living here. To be honest I expected more of Barnsley as a town and a club.' A local Barnsley girl put down her pint long enough to respond in a BBC interview: 'My reaction to his remarks is unprintable. He wants to look in the mirror before talking about us. He's no oil painting.'

French international Youri Djorkaeff had exactly the opposite feelings to Georgi when he joined Bolton Wanderers in February 2002 to help them battle against relegation. He said later in a *Guardian* interview, 'I didn't know what to expect but I was in love with England, in love with its shitty weather, the people, the fans.' Nowadays he's the chief executive officer of the FIFA Foundation charity, but when he was growing up he was a Liverpool fan. 'I bought lots of Liverpool shirts and hats all the time – not wearing them, just collecting. I was fascinated by the clubs and the fans.'

The supporters got upset, and then the player got upset, which all goes to prove what we knew already – that football is an emotional game. Arsenal captain Granit Xhaka was substituted during a 2-2 draw with Crystal Palace in October 2019 and he responded angrily when fans cheered the decision. He waved his arms at the crowd, cupped his ears towards them, and tore off his shirt as he reached the tunnel. Manager Unai Emery said, 'His reaction was wrong. We are here because we have supporters. We work for them and need to have respect for them when they are applauding us and criticising us.' On the other hand, another Arsenal player, Nacho Monreal, who moved on after six years at the club, got it spot on when he left: 'I would like to say thank you to all my team-mates and staff, and especially to the fans for all the respect and love they have always shown me. I'll always remember you.'

You don't go to a football match to be hurt by a player but a Newcastle supporter was winded where it hurts most by a flying corner flag kicked by Matt Ritchie in celebration of a goal, while Italy's all-time leading goalscorer Luigi Riva broke the arm of a nine-year-old fan who was standing behind the goal at training, so powerful was his shot. Another supporter, enjoying the game while supporting Northampton Town, was hit by a wayward shot just as he was about to take a swig of his coffee. His mate recalled, 'My abiding memory of that afternoon is this poor, unfortunate fella trying to dry his head and shirt with his handkerchief.' Then there was unlucky young Tony Clarke: 'I was seven and sat on a barrier at Luton in 1990 when John Dreyer twatted me in the face during the warm-up with a shot and I fell back off the barrier. He came to check I was okay and then again after the match and gave me his shirt.'

I'm not an idiot, I'm deluded, said the Newcastle fan in the opening chapter in defence of his commitment to being a supporter. The same might be said of the only fan of Swedish league side Gefle IF who attended a midweek away match which involved a 700-mile round trip. The players made a point of thanking him personally for his devotion afterwards.

When a footballer stops to top up with petrol, or pops down to the corner shop to see what mark out of ten a newspaper has given him, there's a risk of running into a fan. I once saw one of my favourite ever players, Rio Ferdinand, out and about in a suburban street. Being polite and respecting his privacy, I declined to make eye contact and pretended not to notice him. But when I sneaked a look, he was giving my wife a lovely smile and respectful good morning. She said as we walked on 'he was very nice' while not having the faintest idea who he was. So I knew who he was but ignored him, while she didn't know but got a greeting she's always remembered. What's that all about?

Rio himself says he likes meeting fans and recalls in his book, *Rio My Story*, 'It's one of the rewards when fans come up for autographs and a chat and appreciate me as a good footballer. And I like the fact I can make people happy just signing a shirt or having a photograph taken with them. When someone comes up to me and says "well done", it's a good feeling. Even if someone says, "Oi, you're shit," I don't mind it too much because at least they have an interest in the game.' Having read that, I realise I should have said to Rio, 'Oi, you're shit,' when I saw him in the street and he would have been pleased about it.

When Tony Cascarino went north of the border and signed for Celtic he knew that one of the world's fiercest rivalries meant he was in danger of confrontation if ever he ventured out in Glasgow. In his book, *Full Time: The Secret Life of Tony Cascarino*, he tells the following story: 'One afternoon I was out shopping with my pregnant wife and my son when a supporter stopped me in the street and offered a critical assessment. "You're fucking shit, you," he hissed, "you're a useless big bastard." Friends had warned me not to react when approached by Rangers fans but this fellow was absolutely raving. "You're a fucking wanker, a useless bastard." "Look mate," I pleaded, "give me a break. Can't you see I'm out with my wife and son?" "You're fucking shit," he said. "And I'm a Celtic fan."'

Vinnie Jones didn't like being recognised in the street when he was a player. But then again he didn't like it when he wasn't recognised. He said in his autobiography, *Vinnie*, 'When I walk down the high street I do get that goldfish feeling, everybody staring, wanting your attention, and your time. Sometimes it's too much for me, I get uptight and find myself being rude to people, telling them to leave me alone. But if I walked down the street and nobody recognised me I would feel so insecure.'

Fat chance of seeing Paul Gascoigne out in the street, particularly after Italia '90 when he was at the height of his fame and popularity. He complained, 'It gets to something when my mates have got to hide me in the boot of a car to get me in and out of my home and the ground – what's the use of being famous if you can't go anywhere without being besieged by people, or you can't get to sleep?'

Players think of supporters as idiots, said Rick Gekoski in his book, *Staying Up: A Fan Behind the Scenes in the Premiership*, and quotes one Coventry player as saying, 'Most of the fans are sad. They think the game is more important than it is, it says something about the miserable kind of lives they lead. They get things out of proportion.'

Twitter was still pretty new back in 2011, but comments on it got right up the nose of West Ham defender Danny Gabbidon after his team had lost and come in for some online criticism. 'U know what,' he tweeted in response, 'you will never get another tweet from me again.' It was probably when he put 'fuck the lot of you' that the FA decided to intervene and fined him £6,000.

The fan who hurled a coin at Liverpool's Jamie Carragher during a contentious FA Cup tie at Arsenal in January 2002 couldn't have expected to ever see it again. But Carragher picked it up and threw it back into the crowd, getting a red card for his actions as well as picking up a £40,000 fine from his club. He also received a formal police warning, an investigation having ended when two fans who claimed they were hit by the coin subsequently refused to take the matter further. Carragher apologised immediately for his actions, which followed Arsenal's Denis Bergkamp getting sent off for a foul on him.

Talking of coin-throwing, and because this story was cut out of a newspaper many years ago, it must be true. The report said that at an FA Cup tie at Arsenal a large group of away fans were making merry by bombarding the police cordon with coins. 'Move about,' shouted a supporter, 'make it 'ard for us!'

So upset at being on the losing Everton side to Liverpool in the 1989 FA Cup Final, Pat Nevin immediately gave his runners-up medal to a fan. So what did the recipient do with it? Display it on his wall? Keep it for his grandchildren? Sell it? No, he kindly posted it back to Nevin as he imagined it had been given away in a fit of anger which would later be regretted. Scotland international Nevin told *The Times*, 'I never had a huge affection for any of my medals.'

15

Non-league:
Did you come in a taxi?

NON-LEAGUE FOOTBALL has the advantage that you can stand (admittedly, a bit of an old-fashioned sort of advantage) and be up close to the action by leaning on the hoardings next to the pitch itself. As long as there isn't too much of a crowd that day, or as long as you get there in good time to grab such a coveted place.

But there's so much else going for it as well. Here's what one non-league fan outlined as the benefits: 'Choose having a drink and a chat with the players after the game. Mix with the opposition fans. The old dears in the tea hut serving Bovril for the 49th consecutive season. Meat raffles. Watch football alongside dogs. Away days in towns you didn't know existed. Get a beer for a couple of quid and stand on the terraces with it. Choose to give your money to a local club not a soulless corporation. Players who know the fans by name. Park right next to the ground. Stand wherever you want. Listen to everything the benches say to the players. Pay a pound for a cup of tea. Proper pies. Honest football right on your doorstep.'

I was lucky enough to spend a lot of my newspaper career writing reports on football matches from international and Premier League level down to non-league. And enjoying it, too. But there were times when that wasn't part of my job, and I would invariably still choose to head off to watch a non-league game. Less hassle. Cheaper to get in. Leave home later and still, as the enthusiastic fan says above, get a parking spot near the ground. I like the atmosphere and sharing the occasion with familiar faces and I like that in hundreds and hundreds of games I've seen I can only ever recall actual physical trouble with any opposition fans just the once. And that was a good many years ago.

As for the standard, the higher the level of football the better and more skilful the player. But I've seen international matches that can be boring, and at non-league level the effort, intensity and determination are almost always there. Personally, if the team I've gone to watch put in 100 per cent effort and have tried their hardest then I don't mind much if they lose to better opponents. I know not everyone thinks that way, and I can certainly remember a game a season or two back when I really loved a 1-0 home win, the only goal of the game scored by a right-back who shouldn't have been anywhere near the opposition goal at the time. I'm not sure the victory was deserved, but never mind, it felt really good.

There's also the benefit that you can wander around in most non-league grounds, change ends at half-time, and take up a different place to get a different view. And you can go and stand with someone you like talking to – or walk away from someone you don't. As season ticket holders at Premier League grounds know, you've got no choice who you get to sit next to. I know a fan who loved football but gave up going because the man in front used to annoy him so much with his insults and criticisms. And they were just the ones he shouted at his own team.

I think of all the things listed previously, many non-league fans relish most of all that the players share the bar with them afterwards and treat them as equals. That the players know them by name and respect them. I was told a story by Paul Joines, a supporter of non-league club Sittingbourne. He was behind the goal with his family and his mates as the substitutes kicked a ball around in front of them at half-time. A misplaced shot by one of the club's favourite ever players, Hicham Akhazzan, soared over the bar and knocked a drink out of the hand of Paul's young son. The player responsible immediately ran off to the dressing room, got £5 out of his wallet, and returned to give it to the young lad by way of an apology. Paul said, 'To this day my son remembers what happened and the player that did it. And whenever they saw each other afterwards they'd have a laugh and joke about it. To me that's the true meaning of grassroots football.'

I was at White Hart Lane in the early 1990s and watched as Paul Gascoigne stripped off the shellsuit-style jacket he'd been wearing in the warm-up and ran across to a lad in a wheelchair and gave it to him. The Spurs crowd roared their approval of a touching moment. Two nice stories and two obviously kind-hearted footballers, but the difference is that the jacket wasn't even Gazza's to give away, while Akhazzan had probably just donated the whole match fee he'd have got for being an unused sub for a non-league club.

And talking of getting to meet the players, what a day it was for Dave Roberts, author of *The Bromley Boys*, his warm account of when he was just 14 and a diehard fan of his local Isthmian League club. Having hitchhiked his way to a night match at Grays in Essex he was offered a lift home by one of the players who just happened to be one of his biggest heroes in the team. Dave remembered, 'I felt as though I was in a dream. Barely able to believe what was happening, my breathing became shallow. He even asked me if I was all right and I assured him I was. He kindly dropped me off right outside my house and I thanked him loudly just in case anyone heard.'

The experiences of another fan, Greg Barber, are also well worth taking on board. He said, 'I have turned my back on the big leagues and now watch local football. Myself and a few friends support Whyteleafe in Surrey. We know our players aren't great, but most are only on about £50–£80 a week, so at least we know that if they have a bad game, they are still trying their hardest. Sometimes, just sometimes, we get our rewards. We have even started to take our young family along as the atmosphere is friendly and safe. We can also use the clubhouse, so we can talk to players, and officials, and even so-called rival fans. Only last year a referee came into the bar, bought us all a drink, then explained why he hadn't given us a penalty. You don't get that in the Premier League.'

It's not just players and the odd generous referee that the fans can rub shoulders with, but also the people who run the club. And you don't get that in the Premier League. Of course, the chairman, secretary and directors are just normal fans like the rest of us, but with more responsibility for making the whole thing work. Usually, they'll be ready and willing to have a chat and listen patiently to the odd unsolicited opinion. Though it has to be pointed out the fans at one particular non-league club call themselves the mushrooms, as they're always kept in the dark.

In the 1980s Glasgow Celtic fans decided they wanted to support an English non-league team when they didn't have a game to watch back in Scotland. Their criteria in choosing a club was that they must wear hoops and must have Celtic in their name. Northern Premier League side Stalybridge Celtic fitted both criteria. The Scottish faithful would arrive in what was called 'very good spirits' and make more noise than any fans before and after at the club's ground in Greater Manchester. They were loved by locals for their good humour and friendship. And their contribution to the bar takings, no doubt.

Meanwhile, Dutch football followers reckoned England was like the promised land for football so they arranged a weekend away – to watch Yorkshire non-league side North Ferriby United. One of them, Jeroen Koot, said, 'Most of us are Feyenoord fans, and a few years ago when there was a decline in European away trips we decided to look for other matches abroad. At Premier League matches, a group of fans from abroad is not such a big deal. The football is great, but you are one of many. At non-league level, support and money at the bar is very important and you feel much appreciated.'

Staying safe from the coronavirus was more important than football, but it was a great shame for Gloucester City when the National League North 2020/21 season was terminated in February while they were top of the table. A fan's poignant Facebook post on Lost Football Grounds and Terraces in the UK told the story: 'When I lived there I went to watch the local non-league team Gloucester City; great outfit and great support. Supporters I now class as proper friends … friends for life. It was hard to watch the floods in 2008 and the ground went literally under water up to the crossbar. For years they played their home games all over the place but no matter where they played a strong following went. Eventually they got their wish and were back home in Gloucester with a new stadium to be proud of. Top of the league in 2020/21 and promotion looking likely and then the season was called null and void because of the virus. What a shame.'

Getting close to the action by leaning over the barriers to watch a match can have its drawbacks. I was at a Maidstone United match once and watched as a defender called James Campbell shaped up to pass the ball back to his goalkeeper. Fatally, well not quite but it felt like it at first, he changed his mind at the last moment and whacked the ball out for a throw-in instead. From a distance of all of ten yards it hit me square in the face and knocked me over.

Scrabbling around on the ground, I made sure my head hadn't fallen off along with my rather smart cap. I retrieved the cap and made the sort of gesture you do after missing a bus you'd run to catch and then pretended you didn't want to get on anyway. 'It's nothing, I'm all right, no need to panic,' I was about to say to the group of concerned well-wishers who had surrounded me and wanted to make sure I hadn't been knocked unconscious. I looked up. Nobody had moved. They all had their backs to me. Everyone was still watching the match as if nothing had happened. My nose throbbed for days afterwards and I never took my eyes off James Campbell again in case he changed his mind about what he was going to do.

It's a big learning curve for goalkeepers in non-league football as they become very aware of what's being said about them from just behind. Blackpool keeper Chris Maxwell quickly discovered one of the perils of stepping down a couple of levels when he went out on loan to Connah's Quay Nomads in Wales: 'You think you'll have a break from the abuse when you change ends at half-time, but the fans follow you from end to end and the abuse carries on!'

One non-league fan decided it was a good idea to take his pet Alsatian with him to a match. But the referee at the United Counties League fixture between Leicester Nirvana and GNG Oadby Town didn't agree. With more than 80 minutes played and Nirvana leading 2-1, the ref abandoned the match because he decided the dog on the sidelines was too big a risk while it was jumping up at the barrier to bark at the players.

At least the Alsatian stayed the right side of the fence – a match between non-league clubs Ilkley Town and Carlton Athletic had to be halted when an alpaca strolled on to the pitch. A Carlton fan said the alpaca, who is known as Oscar, was a regular at matches and had invaded the pitch in protest at some of the referee's decisions.

Talking of pets at games, a Hertfordshire Senior Centenary Trophy quarter-final was stopped by the referee because a fan's pet Senegal parrot kept imitating the noise of his whistle. Ref Gary Bailey told *The Guardian*, 'I've never known anything like it. This woman was standing right by the touchline and suddenly unveiled a cage with this big green parrot in it. I didn't mind at first. But then every time I blew my whistle the bird made exactly the same sound. It was bizarre. The crowd were all laughing. In the end, there was only one thing for it.' He showed the owner a metaphorical red card and asked her to leave and take her parrot with her.

When non-league side Marine FC were drawn at home to mighty Spurs in the third round of the 2020/21 FA Cup and coronavirus restrictions meant they couldn't admit fans, they announced that all Spurs season ticket holders will be given free entry to a Marine league game the following season as compensation. I hope there's a big take-up on the Merseyside club's tongue-in-cheek offer.

To recoup some of the inevitable losses from what they could have got that day, Marine came up with the bright idea of selling £10 virtual tickets which included a raffle with a prize of becoming the team's manager for a friendly game. Spurs manager José Mourinho was among the 30,697 who purchased a ticket. Further help came from a local resident and regular supporter, the former Liverpool and England international Jamie Carragher.

He sponsored the dugouts and pre-match warm-up tops through his charity, the JC23 Foundation. Incidentally, Marine have a good way of knowing which neighbour's door to knock on to get their ball back when it goes over the fences surrounding their pitch. They've painted the house numbers on each fence so they know which one to go to. Ingenious, eh? There's plenty of non-league grounds I've been to where that would be a good idea to copy.

It wasn't uncommon once for top players to end their careers in non-league – perhaps for the comparatively modest money, or just for the love of playing football. Jimmy Case won three European Cups in an illustrious career with Liverpool but I remember seeing him one Monday night ploughing through mud and rain at Hednesford when he was nearly 40 and briefly turning out in the Southern League. And he didn't cut corners, putting in as much effort and commitment as anyone on the field. More than some, probably.

In his autobiography, *Hard Case*, he remembers that it wasn't all glamour and glory, even in his illustrious Liverpool days. During a break in play a fan once offered him his pie. 'I took a big bite out of it, much to the amazement of the rest of the crowd, who loved it,' Case wrote. Much as there is to admire in Jimmy's get-stuck-in attitude – and who doesn't love a pie? – I'd still like to hear this story from the fan's point of view as well. For a start, what was he doing in possession of an uneaten pie? Surely we always eat our packed lunch the minute we get in the ground, and don't wait for the players to come out? And what did he do with it once a large chunk had been bitten out by hungry Case? Nibble round the edges? Show it to his mates? Or save it until Instagram had been invented so he could put up a picture of a half-eaten pie?

Talking of pies, Tom Piper tells the story of a match he was at when three large lads were met by opposition supporters with that old favourite chant of 'Who ate all the pies?' When one of the same big boys was spotted on his own taking his place for the second half they altered the taunt to 'Who ate both his mates?'

And one final thought on the undoubted pleasure of being a fan of non-league football, offered up by Clive's tweet: 'Wandered past Fleet Town FC today. A picturesque, friendly and peaceful place to watch football.' If the sound of that floats your boat, then Fleet's not unique in non-league football for those serene-sounding qualities.

16

Managers: You're getting sacked in the morning

IT WAS every supporter's dream. Steve Davies was just standing there moaning at his team – as you do – when he was invited to go on as a substitute and see if he could do any better. It was only a friendly, but West Ham fanatic Steve jumped at the chance. What a thrill, what a once-in-a-lifetime moment.

It was a pre-season friendly in 1994 at Oxford City, with West Ham under the management of larger-than-life Harry Redknapp. Steve and his mates Chunk and Bazza had taken up places near the dugout and started dishing out some stick. Mixed with constructive advice, obviously.

In his autobiography, *Always Managing*, Redknapp takes up the story: 'He wasn't nasty, there was no foul language, and every spare inch of him was covered in West Ham tattoos so I could see he loved the club. I turned round to big mouth and said, "You've got some bunny, can you play as good as you talk?" He said he was better than

Lee Chapman so I told him he was on. I thought I'd make his day.' As a typical Redknapp aside, he explains in the book how he was then asked the name of his new substitute by the Oxford PA announcer. 'Didn't you watch the World Cup?' I asked. 'That's Tittishev of Bulgaria.' 'Oh yes,' he said, nodding wisely. 'I thought it was him.'

Many years later, Steve gave an interview which appeared in *The Guardian* and he relived that wonderful day again. He said, 'I thought Harry was having a laugh with me. I didn't think I was actually going to get on, or I thought I might get a minute or two as a joke.' Steve thought he'd scored in the 71st minute and celebrated wildly but it was ruled out for offside. Playing for West Ham was still the greatest moment of his life but he admitted that after that non-goalscoring high point he ran out of energy. After all, he'd been smoking a fag and considering his third beer of the day when Harry made the unexpected invitation to get stuck in. And he was, by his own admission, just a pub footballer at best. The writer of the newspaper story about that memorable day, Jeff Maysh, spent years tracking Steve down before they finally met. When Steve asked him why, the journalist replied, 'I explained that his story is an allegory for hope.'

Some might have thought this should have been the other way round, but two of the Nottingham Forest fans who were hit by the club's manager, Brian Clough, during a 1989 pitch invasion went back the next day and apologised for their actions. A few dozen happy Forest fans ran on to the pitch after seeing their team beat QPR 5-2. Never the most predictable of men, Clough got enraged and started dragging them off and cuffing a few round the ears while he was at it. He said afterwards he regretted his actions and it's even said there was some kissing taking place when the apologies were delivered.

Clough always had something of a love-hate relationship with supporters and Duncan Hamilton had another story to tell about him in his terrific book, *Provided You Don't Kiss Me*. A supporter passing by in the car park once offered a bit of unsolicited advice to the manager. Hamilton said, 'He had rows of enamel badges pinned on both lapels and the end of his Forest scarf, which suggested he was a veteran of European Cup campaigns. He clearly thought he was making a shrewd and unhostile remark but Clough gave him a two-minute lecture in reply. His final line was, "Go home and lose some weight. Next time, be more respectable."'

If he had a love-hate relationship with supporters then Clough was no different with his players. Lee Chapman, before later joining West Ham and being replaced by a fan, once scored four goals in a match for Forest and expected a great reception from the manager when he went in the dressing room afterwards. 'Eh, Chapman,' shouted Clough, 'when you score a hat-trick you run over to me, not the supporters. I'm the one who signed you.' Former Forest lynchpin centre-half Larry Lloyd said of Clough, 'As a manager there's no limit to my respect for him, but as a man he's not my cup of tea. I once told him I'd never be caught standing at a bar having a drink with him. He said I shouldn't worry because the feeling was mutual!'

He was mentioned previously but one privileged fan was allowed access behind the scenes of a top-flight club for the whole of the 1997/98 season and then wrote a book about it, *Staying Up: A Fan Behind the Scenes in the Premiership*. It was, as they say, warts and all stuff. So much so that Gordon Strachan, manager of the club in question, Coventry City, told the author, Rick Gekoski, 'If I had known you were going to write this sort of book, I never would have allowed you access to myself or the team. Having said that, I think it's one of the best books about football ever written.'

With spectacularly poor foresight, Manchester United manager Ron Atkinson promised that the 1985 FA Cup Final would be a Wembley classic at the end of what had been a horrible season to try to restore some badly needed faith in besieged English football. 'The game needs a lift,' he reckoned, after all sorts of tragedies and hooligan behaviour. But it all went wrong as the match will be best remembered as the first final in which a player was sent off. And it was a United player, too, Kevin Moran, who provoked further criticism for trying to argue the decision with the referee. He was later exonerated from blame for the so-called professional foul that got him sent off, and was belatedly presented with his winner's medal.

I knew larger-than-life Atkinson back in the 1970s when he was in charge at Cambridge United, his first job as a manager. He used to come into the local newspaper offices once a month to judge a competition for 'best performance by a local football club'. Big Ron summed up his commitment to his role as a judge: 'I don't mind who wins, you choose,' he'd say, settling back in his chair. 'I'll have two sugars in my tea and I'll tell you some of my stories.' And he did. I loved one of the quotes Ron was credited with later in his career: 'I never comment on referees and I'm not going to break the habit for that prat.'

How not to go about winning over the hearts and minds of your own fans. From 1985 for eight years Barnet had a chairman in Stan Flashman, who said in a radio interview, 'The supporters don't matter as far as I'm concerned. They just pay their entrance fee. I don't care whether they come to Barnet or not.' He left soon afterwards, having established a record by apparently sacking charismatic manager Barry Fry seven times during his stay there. The stories are told in Tony Thornton's book *The Club That Wouldn't Die* in which he also says that Flashman's resignation as chairman was announced on 1 April 1993, and supporters assumed it was just an April Fool's joke.

Not many football club managers have ever paid for four tubas to be repaired, but that's what Barnsley boss Valérien Ismaël did in 2021. He found out that Barnsley Brass, a band that's made music in the town for more than 100 years, needed help with £200 of repairs to instruments. He settled the bill and also donated to a foodbank having previously sent Christmas cards to the club's young supporters. The Frenchman also did the right thing by setting up home in the heart of Barnsley when he took over as manager, rather than commuting in from somewhere thought of as more desirable.

And talk about being close to the community – both Scotland manager Jock Stein and England's Graham Taylor were spotted back in the day on the terraces, mixing happily with the fans while they watched potential new players. What with 99 per cent of scouting now done online, that's definitely a relic of the past we'll never see again.

No one can be a football manager and escape criticism. If you can't stand the heat get out of the kitchen, so the saying goes, and managers are moaned at from all directions – by the fans, the players (behind their back, of course), the media and the people upstairs who run the clubs. I saw a tweet about Spurs manager José Mourinho during the 2020/21 season from Shay which said, 'I was fully behind José and the idea of winning trophies under him. I was even willing to put up with his defensive style of play but I didn't expect it to be THIS bad. It's awful, it's depressing and it's definitely the worst football I have ever seen Spurs play.' Say it like you think, Shay.

TV and radio presenter Jeremy Vine was much more subtle in his criticism of Mourinho at the end of the manager's two controversial spells in charge of Chelsea. Vine, a long-term season ticket holder at Stamford Bridge, demonstrated a classic PCP technique. If you want to have a go at someone then praise them first and praise them last, and put the criticism in the middle. Otherwise known as a shit sandwich.

Vine's letter was reproduced on a BBC site so he can't have intended his opinions to stay private. He started nicely: 'You have never met me, but every week I sit with my daughter directly above your position in the Stamford Bridge dugout. Your intensity is incredible and I love the sense of danger you bring to every waking moment. You always reminded me of the most popular boy at school: people would do anything to be his friend, and your players would do anything to impress you.'

So Vine built Mourinho up with praise and then stuck the knife in with his criticism of the manager for the way he had clashed with the Chelsea team doctor: 'She was popular; the players sided with her against you; you lost the dressing room. You caused the doctor to leave and the players sacked you. Do you understand that, José? You were fired by your own players.'

But, as we now know what to expect, there was praise at the end again from Vine: 'We will now get a sane, sober-suited manager, and it will not be the same. If one day you regret what happened, rest assured that there's a father who got to spend precious afternoons with his young daughter because she wanted to be taken to Chelsea and watch your magic and madness unfold on the green in front of her.'

Mourinho himself is no stranger to the old-fashioned skill of letter-writing demonstrated here by Vine – when he was Manchester United manager he sent a lovely little one to a 94-year-old lifetime fan who was recovering from a stroke. He told Fredrick Schofield, 'I just wanted to write to you to thank you for your loyal support and devotion to the club. The enthusiasm of the fans continues to astound me. We are all thinking of you.'

No wonder the man has inspired so much love and criticism from fans, probably in equal measures, wherever he's been.

17

Celebrities: Bring me sunshine

IT MIGHT be quicker to list the celebrities who don't have a favourite football team. This chapter is packed with those who do, and to be fair they're proper fans and not just supporters in name who think it looks cute or fashionable on a CV to list 'football fan' in among their hobbies.

Let's start with Frank Skinner, not because he's the most famous celebrity talked about in this chapter, and not just because I've always been a fan and have seen his live act a few times. No, it's because he did much to restore football to its rightful place in English hearts in the 1990s. We've seen how many disasters and horrific stories marred the '80s but along came Skinner, and his mate David Baddiel, with their *Fantasy Football League* TV show. They found things to laugh about, people to mock, iconic moments to re-enact. He and Baddiel also wrote the once-in-a-lifetime football anthem 'Three Lions' – along with The Lightning Seeds – which became the only song ever to have four separate stints at number one in the UK singles chart with the same artistes. I remember the TV camera lingering on Skinner before an England match when he was enthusiastically joining in with his own song on the PA, backed for the occasion by a choir of 80,000 people. If we ever ignore or forget that the world of football should be fun and entertaining then we're poorer for it.

Football fanatic Skinner has always strongly advocated that everyone should support their local team, the one nearest to where they were born. So as a passionate West Bromwich Albion follower he wanted to practise what he preached and was keen for his baby to be born at nearby Sandwell General Hospital. Trouble is, he lived in London at the time and his girlfriend wasn't very keen on a 120-mile dash when she was about to give birth. Skinner told the *Birmingham Mail*, 'She thought I'd got my priorities wrong!' The baby boy – they called him Buzz after the astronaut Buzz Aldrin – was born in London.

Skinner writes about being a besotted football fan in his book *On the Road*. He says, 'Those who hear football's music place it at the centre of their lives; those who don't often think it just promotes violence, idolatry and tribalism. Those criticisms have validity, but they really aren't the whole picture. The problem is that it's impossible to explain why football is magical, because the place where it touches you is some highly charged emotional mystery zone where words feel a bit pedestrian. I'm aware of the bad stuff, but its significance seems to dissolve in that zone. It's probably all to do with the unfathomability of love.'

All quite heavy from someone who's made a lifetime's career out of being humorous. I'm sure he's said more amusing things but I love to recall when Cameroon picked Rigobert Song in their midfield for a 1994 World Cup match and Skinner solemnly showed the team sheet to Baddiel, saying, 'Look, they're playing R Song!'

I reckon the funniest man there's ever been, though, was Eric Morecambe and what a day it was in 2014 when Morecambe met Luton Town, the two football clubs in his life, and competed for a trophy which bore his name.

Eric Morecambe was born in, well, Morecambe and took his stage name from his home town. The football club's old stadium could be seen from his childhood home and he was a regular on the terraces. Not only that, he was a good player himself, according to his son Gary, talking to the *Lancashire Post*. 'He was a left-winger and had a very powerful left foot, I know that. We used to play in the back garden and he was always Pelé or Bobby Charlton.'

In 1959 Eric was invited to become president of Morecambe FC and though it was a bit of a figurehead role he took it seriously and continued to support the club even at the height of his hugely successful show business career in partnership with Ernie Wise. His nephew Michael Threlfall said, 'He would stand and watch with his coat collar pulled up around his face and would say to me, "Now let me watch the game, Michael, don't go telling your mates that I'm here!"'

When he moved south to Hertfordshire, he still loved his football and began to take son Gary to Kenilworth Road to watch Luton Town. Eric went on to become a director of the club, and subsequently vice-president, and a club lounge is named after him. Meanwhile, back home,

Morecambe has a lovely statue of him on the seafront, and the trophy his two clubs contested is a replica of it.

Eric died at the young age of 58 in 1984 following a heart attack but would have loved to know that his favourite football result, which he often joked about, actually occurred in 2018. It was East Fife 4 Forfar 5 and was the score on penalties after the clubs drew with each other in a Scottish League Cup tie. He would have adjusted his glasses, pulled a silly face, and had a lot of fun with that one.

For most fans, running their childhood club would be a dream come true. So much so for Elton John that he did it twice. The legendary musician was brought up near Watford and followed the club as a child. Football ran in the family; his cousin Roy Dwight played for Nottingham Forest in the 1959 FA Cup Final and broke his leg as well as scoring a goal. Though not in that order.

After becoming a director and chairman in 1976, Elton supervised Watford soaring up through three divisions to finish second to Liverpool in the First Division in 1983 and reaching the FA Cup Final the following year. He sold the club after 11 years, but was still standing and stayed as president. Then he bought it back for another five years at the helm.

The all-round superstar reckoned that the opening of the Elton John Stand in 2014 was one of the greatest days of his life – and his lifelong love affair with Watford continues to this day. But he's not so keen on going to matches any more as fans and their mobiles have put him off. He told the *Watford Observer*, 'I don't like crowds and you're having your photo taken all the time these days. It's not so easy to relax and just concentrate on the game.'

It seems only right that the rebellious Gallagher brothers should be involved in turning on its head the tradition of following family history over which team they choose to support. Noel explained, 'My dad hated his brothers who were all Manchester United supporters so he chose City just to piss them off. No other reason than that. Liam and I should by rights have been United fans.'

As all of football knows, the Oasis boys stuck with their dad's choice and have been high-profile and fervent City supporters all their lives. No back seat for them. Noel has been friends with many of the players as well as manager Pep Guardiola and he was on the pitch celebrating with them when City won the Premier League title in 2018. And when the club previously claimed the championship in 2012 with that dramatic late Sergio Agüero goal against QPR. Noel remembered in an interview with *Goal*, 'I swore a lot and then I cried like a baby. I've never seen anything like that before. It was mind-blowing.'

Aston Villa's famous fans range from Lennie Godber and Frank Pike to the Duke of Cambridge and Tom Hanks. For the benefit of young readers, Godber (*Porridge*) and Pike (*Dad's Army*) were characters in TV sitcoms back in comedy's halcyon days of the 1970s. I had to look up the dates as I couldn't believe it was that long ago. Anyway, both were Aston Villa fans in their respective much-loved roles and wore claret-and-blue scarves to prove it.

The amazingly talented Hanks is a more recent football convert, but at least he's actually seen Villa play. He told the BBC he was once listening to the football results when working in England. 'I didn't know where any of these places were and then I heard them say Aston Villa,' said Hanks. 'And I thought what a lovely spot. It's a beautiful villa, you throw open the French doors and there's the beautiful port of Aston down below you.' He wasn't exactly spot on with his vision but he's stayed loyal and has waved the club claret-and-blue in the air on the odd red carpet.

Prince William was more pragmatic in his choice. He told Gary Lineker for a BBC interview, 'At school I got into football big time but I didn't want to follow all my friends who were Man United or Chelsea fans. I wanted to have a team that was more mid-table, that could give me more rollercoaster moments. I chose Aston Villa and really felt the atmosphere and camaraderie was something I could connect with. Also I was born in 1982, when they won the European Cup, so the history and pedigree around Villa has always been quite close to me.'

Port Vale fan Robbie Williams put his money where his mouth is when he bought shares worth £240,000 in the club in 2006. Born just a two-minute walk from the ground, the former Take That star was all set to perform on his beloved team's Vale Park in 2020 – as a singer, not a footballer – but coronavirus forced a postponement of his concert.

Not many Everton fans would have turned down the chance to appear in a film with Rocky. The Oscar-nominated Sylvester Stallone, already an Everton fan having previously made an appearance on the Goodison Park pitch, played Rocky Balboa again in a spin-off film called *Creed* which also featured lifelong Everton fan and boxer Tony Bellew. It was Bellew who asked Everton fans before a match in 2015 to help with a scene for the film. 'Go absolutely nuts at half-time,' he asked them. 'Be sure you make as much noise as possible to help us create a brilliant atmosphere. I know what kind of noise Evertonians create – it will be perfect for the scene.'

Stallone, who also starred as John Rambo in his stellar Hollywood career, had been to the ground in 2007 at the invitation of a friend, club director Robert Earl. Sly went on the pitch and waved his scarf to the crowd while pumping a fist in the direction of the Gwladys Street end. He was in the UK to promote the sixth film in the *Rocky* series and said later he regretted not trying to buy the club at that time. He was on rocky ground when he then claimed he wouldn't be able to afford it any more.

Stallone is not the only superstar Everton fan – Paul McCartney is a blue, though, to be fair, he also supports Liverpool. He told Tribuna.com, 'Here's the deal – my father was born in Everton, my family are officially Evertonians, so they're my team. But I met Kenny Dalglish after a concert at Wembley Arena and I thought, you know what, I'm just going to support them both because it's all Liverpool. That's it, they're both great teams. When people ask me how I can support them both I say I have special dispensation from the Pope.'

No problem for actor, comedian and travel documentary maker Michael Palin in having two different teams to support. Since he was a boy he's been a loyal Sheffield United fan, but if their big rivals, Sheffield Wednesday, are in town he'll go and support them instead. In an interview with the magazine *When Saturday Comes* he reflected on what it's like to be a fan these days: 'The afternoon is geared more to the spectators than it used to be. You can get a better view of the game, it's a more comfortable experience in general but I worry about the commercial pressures coming in from people buying clubs just to sell them on.'

Oscar-winning actress Margot Robbie is a Fulham fan because of her husband Tom's allegiance to the club – he's English film director Tom Ackerley. An excited Fulham supporter was only slightly carried away with finding out about that when he tweeted, 'When you think you couldn't love Margot Robbie any more she comes out with this.'

Ray Winstone has usually played hard men in films and TV throughout his long career, but he showed a softer side in writing the foreword to an autobiography, *Scoring: An Expert's Guide*, by his mate, former West Ham and Scotland striker Frank McAvennie. West Ham fanatic Winstone wrote, 'When their team is playing well the lives of football supporters soar. It's the perfect happy pill and no harmful side effects. Well not many. Sad bastards? Maybe, but I like it.' He also gave an interesting glimpse of what he wants from a match when he spoke to talkSPORT in 2020. He said, 'When your players walk on to that pitch with a smile on their face, you know you've got half a chance. To me it doesn't matter if you don't win … if the players are out there giving it 100 per cent then that means the world to me. It's not about going out and winning 1-0.'

Comedian Bob Mortimer is a Middlesbrough fan who saw his first game at their former ground, Ayresome

Park, when he was seven and Italy were playing North Korea in a 1966 World Cup group match. He said, 'I loved that ground. And the journey to it, full of hope, and the first look at the pitch from the top of the steps. It's my superstition now when I go to the Riverside to always take the same photo of the ground the moment I sit in my seat. And if I'm watching them play on TV, I'll always go to the toilet if we're in desperate need of a goal.'

Actor Idris Elba revealed his football loyalties in reply to a question on Twitter in 2014. 'I'm a Gooner, bruvva,' he said. And he proved it a few years later when he featured in a promotional video for Adidas to reveal a new Arsenal kit. In the video, which also included former player Ian Wright, Elba claimed he could have played for Arsenal. He commented, 'I'm a big believer in the power of football to change lives.'

As a young actor, Richard Attenborough trained with Chelsea's players to prepare for a film role, but he was already a fan of the club and spent his whole life as a dedicated supporter. An Oscar-winning director, Lord Attenborough was honoured by being given the role of Chelsea's life president. He died in 2014 at the age of 90.

Like so many of us as it's turned out, Sir Patrick Stewart was first taken to a football match when he was seven years old. And for more than 70 years since he's been a devoted follower of his local club, Huddersfield. The *Star Trek* star, who has had a long and successful career in films, on stage and on TV, said in an interview with Sky Sports, 'My Uncle Arnold took me by bus and we stood on the terraces of the old Leeds Road ground. There was something about being in the stadium that I'd never experienced before. I get the same rush when I walk up the steps of any ground, no matter where it is.'

Hollywood megastar Hugh Jackman is the proud owner of a 1985 Norwich City replica shirt in honour of when the club beat Sunderland at Wembley in the final of the Milk Cup, otherwise known as the Football League Cup before sponsorship came along. It's not a random bit of shirt-owning – Hugh's mum Grace comes from Norwich and is a long-time fan of the club. His parents emigrated to Australia in 1967 under the Ten Pound Poms scheme and Hugh was born in Sydney. He's gone on to conquer the world in both singing and acting, but admitted in a 2011 interview with the BBC that he regretted turning down an invitation to become a celebrity investor in Norwich City. 'A big mistake,' he called it.

Another high-profile entertainer who did get involved more deeply with Norwich City is Stephen Fry. The actor/comedian/presenter/writer was brought up in Norfolk and spent five years as a director of City before becoming a club ambassador.

But, of course, Norwich has an even better known celebrity supporter. Anyone who's followed football in the last 15 years or so will recognise the words, 'Where are you? Where are you? Let's be havin' you! Come on!' Yes, that was the screeching request to Norwich fans at half-time in a crucial match with Manchester City in 2005. They were uttered by the club's majority shareholder Delia Smith, the larger-than-life TV cook who also clearly loves her football. Talking about that famous night, Delia said,

'They just handed me the microphone and said "go on, go and do it".' She told the fans, 'A message for the best football supporters in the world: we need a 12th man here.' Her impassioned plea was big news the next day, but the story had a disappointing conclusion for Norwich – they lost 3-2 and were relegated at the end of the season.

Food writer and TV cook Nigella Lawson, also a Chelsea fan, laid bare her love of football in an article for the *London Evening Standard* in 2009. She wrote, 'There is something about football players, that particular mixture of otherness, strength and petulance, that seems to sum up the muscularity and fragility of maleness. It shows men as women see them: competitive, full of greedy ego and with that mummy-watch-me-jump need to impress. I like it when players give a hug to someone on the opposing team after a match, or help one another up after a stumble. And of course, a sense of belonging is such a great part of being a football fan. It allows you to find common ground and have an agreeable and warm chat about sport. Soccer provides the most compelling, most enduring soap opera I know.'

Talking of TV chefs/writers, I sat next to Ainsley Harriott at a wedding a few years ago and we had a nice chat about most things, but nearly all of it sport. He asked me who my favourite ever cricketer was (Alan Knott) and I asked him about his favourite ever footballer. Just like, I suspect, many a lifelong Arsenal fan, his choice was Thierry Henry.

No one dared to tell Mick Hucknall he was overdue on stage for a Simply Red open-air gig because he was busy watching his beloved Manchester United on television.

'They didn't knock because they were frightened to disturb me,' Hucknall told *FourFourTwo*, 'but it's not something I do all the time.' He also revealed that Sir Alex Ferguson had provided him with a nice seat behind the dugout at the Barcelona ground for the 1999 Champions League Final. 'But I didn't go because the last time I went there I travelled with the team and we got absolutely stuffed. I thought if I go again and we lose it will be my fault!'

It was no joking matter but comedians were often big football followers back in the day, and lifelong fan Tommy Trinder led the way by becoming chairman of Fulham for 17 years from 1959. Another funny-man fan, Jasper Carrott, used to include football in his stand-up and once commented, 'David Icke says he's here to save the world, but he saved bugger all when he played in goal for Coventry.' And then there was Norman Wisdom, who was a board member at his local team, Brighton, but spread his favours around as he was also pictured waving to fans from the pitch while dressed in full home kit at both Manchester City and Newcastle. On top of that he made a guest appearance on the pitch in 2001 when England played in Albania, wearing a half-Albanian and half-England shirt. The home crowd already knew and loved Wisdom's comedy and were tickled pink when he did one of his trademark trips on his way out to the centre circle.

Comedian and *Strictly Come Dancing* 2020 winner Bill Bailey found himself living near Queens Park Rangers when he first moved to London – and he's been watching them ever since. 'I like the fact it's a small ground, you are right on top of the pitch and it's right in the middle of a housing area. It felt like what football is meant to be all about.' He also mused about football once in an interview with *FourFourTwo*: 'What intrigues me is the relentless optimism among football fans and I think that is certainly more the case in the lower leagues. There is a tremendous loyalty, which is great to see up close. I realise that it suits me and I know that it's what I've always considered being a football fan is all about.'

The whole of leading theatre and film director Sir Trevor Nunn's professional life has been about creating drama, passion and emotion. He lived out all three when he sat with his dad five rows behind the royal box at Wembley in May 1978 to watch Ipswich Town play Arsenal in the FA Cup Final. Trevor had been a fan of his hometown club Ipswich since his dad first took him when he was just five. His club won the final 1-0 thanks to a Roger Osborne goal. 'When the final whistle blew the two of us just sobbed and sobbed,' said Sir Trevor. 'I've never been so happy in my life.'

Gary Lineker's football career took him all over the world for club and country, but his heart remained very much at home. He was born in Leicester, his first club was Leicester City, and he's always been a big fan. So much so he's been made an honorary vice-president of the club and when Leicester were doing remarkably well in the Premier League in the historic 2015/16 season he promised that if they went on to win the title he would present BBC's *Match of the Day* in just his underpants. Maybe he got carried away in the excitement of the moment, perhaps he was just flying by the seat of his pants, or it might just have been an extra incentive to the team to stay top. Whatever, it worked, and for the first episode of the programme in the following season there was Lineker in all his glory. Well, just his white boxer shorts, anyway. A promise is a promise and Lineker, who won the FIFA Fair Play Award for never getting booked in a career lasting 567 games, had kept his word.

18

Protests: I want to be in that number

LOTS OF clubs have successfully completed moves into new stadiums and apparently carried on as before. West Ham didn't. Fans were vociferously against the move from the well-contained Boleyn Ground to the openness and grandeur of the nearby 2012 London Olympic stadium. Season ticket holder Nigel Kahn started a petition protesting about the move and collected thousands of signatures. He summed up his feeling: 'I'd be happy to leave the Boleyn Ground but only if it was to go to a real football stadium.' Another fan, Rory Sheen, commented, 'Upton Park is a proper old-fashioned ground and a lot of West Ham fans would agree that it's acted as our 12th man.'

The club's board were set on the move, however, and despite ongoing fans' protests, and unrest at some matches, West Ham moved in 2016 to the London Stadium, as it was called by then. Fans staged one final on-pitch demonstration after the very last game at Upton

Park, but within months their much-loved old home had been demolished and redevelopment was immediately under way.

Another club hit by a furious reaction to moving to a new stadium, Brighton had points deducted for pitch invasions in the 1990s as fans marched on in protest at leaving their old Goldstone Ground. When a boycott was called, only a fifth of an average gate of 10,000 turned up for a home match with Mansfield in the 1996/97 season. Then a 'Fans United' day calling on support from all over the country resulted in a full ground and a 5-0 home win. There was also a march and other publicity stunts to keep the protest going. All to no avail as the ground shut in 1997 though many fans apparently boycott the retail centre which now occupies the Goldstone land, and some can't even bring themselves to drive past it. They shared with Gillingham until 1999 and then for a decade they played their home matches at an athletics stadium, never a satisfactory solution for watching football, and visiting fans were taunted with, 'Can you see the game from there?' Scott claimed on Facebook it was so cold and miserable in the away end it was the only football ground he'd been to where he had to dress as if he was going on an expedition on a trawler.

Even so, Brighton's relatively new, splendid-looking Amex Stadium still has its detractors, as they complain it lacks adequate parking and good public transport access. And that's from fans who had to endure loads of years without a ground at all, and had to go 70 miles to watch home games at Gillingham.

Charlton fans spent seven years travelling to other London grounds for home games when The Valley was shut in 1985 for safety reasons. But even after the much-celebrated homecoming, problems off the field continued. In 2016 fans held a mock funeral before a match with Middlesbrough and then threw beach balls on to the pitch to register their disapproval at the controversial owners of the club. And when they were relegated to League One after the last game of that season a flare was thrown on the pitch during the game, and fans invaded it afterwards to stage a demonstration in front of the directors' box.

Back in 1968, when organising a protest would have been so much harder logistically without the internet, Aston Villa fans were fed up with the club's board and performances on the field where the team had just gone bottom of the old Second Division. So a protest meeting was set up and organisers were amazed when about 1,000 people turned up. One of the men behind it, John Russell, later recalled to BirminghamLive that they hadn't really planned what to say at the meeting but just felt the board were out of touch and had lost the plot. He said, 'The sheer number of people at our meeting and our collective frustration was the kick up the backside that they needed. They took it as a signal that perhaps they weren't up to it, which they weren't.' Ownership of the club was subsequently transferred and Villa moved forward again.

But they went backwards in 2016 as the day they were relegated from the Premier Division fans staged a 74th-minute 'celebration' timed to coincide with the club's foundation in 1874. Inflatables including beach balls and – a new one, this – a blow-up doll were thrown on to the pitch and the game had to be temporarily halted. Villa fans said it wasn't a protest but a celebration of their resolve to stick by the club during what had been a very hard season.

Liverpool supporters won a huge battle with their club in February 2016 when about 10,000 of them walked out of a home game with Sunderland in protest. It was the 77th minute of the match and the number was significant as £77 was the higher amount of proposed increased ticket prices for the following season. The club owners said sorry and scrapped the rises. Who would have thought then that five years later those same fans would be so deprived of live action they'd have given almost anything to be in a position to stomp out of a game in protest at anything.

A live chicken dressed in Blackburn club colours wandered on and stopped play during a Premier League match at Ewood Park against Wigan in 2012. It was released by fans in protest at club owners Venky's, whose company is a poultry business. But the owners didn't chicken out and stayed at the helm.

Cardiff City fans organised themselves to stay behind after the 2013 South Wales derby with Swansea and chant 'pro-Blue/anti-Tan' messages. Their target was majority shareholder Vincent Tan whose unpopular decisions included changing the team colours from the traditional blue to red. 'Blue then – Blue now – Blue forever' read one banner. The Bluebirds it is then.

Everton's match with Manchester City in 2012 was halted by a spectator's publicity stunt when he handcuffed himself to a goalpost. It was part of an ongoing campaign against an airline which, he claimed, had unlawfully dismissed his daughter. Bolt cutters were quickly used to free him so the match could resume and the 'fan' was banned from going to football for three years and fined £300.

Not all protesters can afford such a dramatic gesture, but a plane flew over Everton's ground trailing a banner calling for the departure of manager Roberto Martinez during one match near the end of the 2015/16 season. 'Time to go, Roberto' was the message floating in the aptly blue sky. And he did indeed go, soon after. Though within months Martinez took over as manager of the Belgium team and took them to their highest finish in the World Cup – third in 2018.

Manchester City escaped punishment when fans jeered the Champions League anthem in 2015 and held up signs saying 'Boo'. It was in protest at sanctions imposed on the club for breaching Financial Fair Play rules and what was perceived as the authority's failure to properly punish CSKA Moscow for their fans racially abusing City player Yaya Touré. City fans were reported for their noisy behaviour during the anthem at matches with Sevilla, but UEFA general secretary Gianni Infantino stuck up for them and said fans had a right to boo anything they wanted.

Crystal Palace fans organised a protest march in 2009, carrying with them a petition asking for changes in stewarding at Selhurst Park. They told chairman Simon Jordan that fans needed to be respected more, and some were staying away from supporting the club because of overzealous stewarding. Oh, and tickets cost too much as well, they claimed.

There was also a pitch protest by Blackpool fans at the end of the 2014/15 season that resulted in the game with Huddersfield being abandoned. They carried 'Oyston out' banners in a long-standing protest about the way the club was being run.

In more recent times, Ipswich Town players were forced to suspend training in 2021 when protesting supporters threw flares into their training ground; Wigan Athletic fans protested outside the Football League's headquarters after the club had entered administration during the coronavirus pandemic; Newcastle fans staged a protest outside the ground during lockdown at the way their club was being run.

There was also unrest among Leyton Orient supporters before they took the matter into their own hands at the end of the 2016/17 season when the club was relegated out of the Football League for the first time in 112 seasons. Five minutes from the end of that final home game, with Colchester leading Orient 3-1, fans invaded the pitch. The players escaped to the sanctuary of the dressing room, while lots more supporters stayed put in their places with obvious dissent about the chosen method of protest.

It was clear that whatever the best way was for fans to express their displeasure, Orient had suffered a downward spiral under the ownership of Francesco Becchetti and feelings and emotions were running high. The fans on the pitch had been chanting 'Becchetti out' and 'Sit down for the Orient' but they were told the match had already been abandoned. Eventually they had to go home for their dinner and the sit-in ended after an hour or so. Once the pitch had been cleared, it turned out the game hadn't been called off at all and it was finished behind closed doors with Colchester still winning 3-1. The unpopular Becchetti was gone soon after and Orient went on to win their place back in the Football League after two years out.

And now for one story about a player confronted by protesting fans, as opposed to the clubs themselves. Rio Ferdinand was home alone in his Manchester United days watching TV when the front gate buzzer sounded. He could see on camera that there were a couple of United fans outside who asked if he would come out and talk to them. He agreed and politely inquired, 'What the fuck do you want?'

His book, *Rio, My Story*, takes us through what happened next: 'I'd thought there were only two blokes but it turned out there was more than 20 geezers with baseball caps and hoods on. My heart started pumping furiously, it was scary, but I was high on adrenaline and there was no backing down now. They'd been drinking in a nearby pub and I could smell booze on them. I told them to take their hoods off as I wanted to see their faces. They did, after I promised I wouldn't go to the police. They said they wanted to talk about the club's owners and whether I was going to sign a new contract. They were proper United fans, they wouldn't have been at my house otherwise. I understood they were concerned but I still wasn't happy and said, "What if my missus had been here by herself? She'd be shitting herself." Then we heard police car sirens because one of the neighbours had phoned the cops and they ran off, although they did thank me first for having the balls to come out and talk to them!'

19

Music: Let's all have a disco

WHEN SUPER-FAN Jamie Webster wrote the lyrics to 'Allez, Allez, Allez' it's probably fair to say he never imagined the day would come when tears would be pouring down his face as he sang it to a worshipping crowd of 50,000. Or another time when he performed it for the beloved manager of his beloved football club. But dreams come true and Jamie lived out his fantasies as Liverpool marched to European and world club football domination in the late 2010s with his song very much providing the musical accompaniment.

A former electrician and still in his 20s, Jamie transformed an old Italian disco classic which had been knocking around football for years into 'Allez, Allez, Allez'. He achieved it by speeding up the tempo and adding Liverpool-specific lyrics. And once Jamie had played his version to a crowded pub it took off, never to look back. Neither did the team, with the European Champions League and FIFA Club World Cup in 2019 followed by an overdue Premier League championship in the stop-start 2019/20 season.

Looking back at the moment when the song first got taken up by the Anfield terraces, Jamie said later in an interview with *The Guardian*, 'I was like, job done. I've finally learnt how to get a song to the masses. It's like my "Wonderwall".' He performed an emotional rendition of it in front of 50,000 fans in Madrid and had the shock of his life when Jürgen Klopp walked in on his performance at a supporters' club event in the USA during a Liverpool pre-season tour. The manager joined in with the singing and said, 'I love the song and I already liked Jamie before I'd met him.'

Catchy as 'Allez, Allez, Allez' is, popular as it is, Liverpool will always have another song that's even more revered: The wonderful 'You'll Never Walk Alone' is movingly and passionately sung by home fans before games at Anfield. It's been that way since the 1960s and will be for the next 100 years at least.

It's not just because of The Beatles, but Liverpool has always been associated with music. And it was a group who were friendly rivals of the Fab Four, Gerry and the Pacemakers, who released 'You'll Never Walk Alone' as a single in 1963. It had been written by the famous American composers Rodgers and Hammerstein for the musical *Carousel*, and was never envisaged as a pop single. Nor even more so as a football anthem that has often moved many a fan to depths of emotion they didn't know they possessed.

It all started when Gerry Marsden, lead singer of Gerry and the Pacemakers, gave the then Liverpool manager Bill Shankly a copy of the record. A couple of years later Shankly chose it as one of his eight favourite songs for the

BBC radio programme *Desert Island Discs*. That further cemented it in Liverpool folklore, and the rest is history.

Perhaps one of its greatest ever renditions came in 2016 when Borussia Dortmund were the visitors to Anfield for a Europa League fixture. The German club also have a deserved reputation for the passion and loving commitment of their fans, and 'You'll Never Walk Alone' happens to be their club song too. The whole ground uniting to belt out the familiar words provided one of those knee-trembling I-was-there moments.

Incidentally, Liverpool fans recorded the highest decibel level of 97 in a survey of Premier League clubs by Fan Chants in 2011. Manchester United's Old Trafford was second to Anfield for the loudness of singing and chanting with a resounding score of 94.

Across Stanley Park from Anfield, Everton have their own piece of famous music to lift fans from their seats when the players come out. And it also goes right back to the 1960s. It's the theme tune from the TV police drama series *Z Cars* which was set in a fictional town near Everton and also starred a couple of the club's fans. There are no words to sing along to but it's rousing and rallying and Everton fans wouldn't have it any other way. Watford also used the *Z Cars* theme as their introductory music for more than 50 years as the first time they tried it they went on a winning run and decided it must have brought them luck. But more recently they dropped it in favour of an Elton John number.

Another inspiring tune from the 1960s has provided the musical backcloth at Crystal Palace throughout the ensuing half-century. Dave Clark Five's foot-stomping 'Glad All Over' actually knocked The Beatles' 'I Wanna Hold Your Hand' off the number one spot in 1964. London 1 Liverpool 0. Clark himself has played the song at Palace's ground, and the team covered his most famous hit as their then traditional single release in the build-up to the 1990 FA Cup Final.

Across London, West Ham fans have been signing 'I'm Forever Blowing Bubbles' since the 1920s when manager Charlie Paynter introduced it. Like Palace, the players released their own version of it when they reached a cup final, but sales didn't bubble over and it never made number one.

The composer who wrote the music for 'You'll Never Walk Alone', the late Richard Rodgers, also has his work belted out by fans along the M62. 'Blue Moon' was sung by Manchester City fans when they were briefly locked in after a match in 1989 and they liked it so much they've given voice to it ever since.

One song which was written specially for a club and has been sung lustily by fans for 50 or so years is 'Marching On Together'. It was the B side to a single released for Leeds United's 1972 FA Cup Final appearance and has been a fixture ever since. Standing up to sing it, all the more so with defiance in all-seater stadiums, is compulsory.

'Goodnight Irene' is a great tradition with Bristol Rovers fans and when the lad next to me started singing it, to his delight – and astonishment – the whole away terrace of Rovers fans immediately joined in. His eyes shining, he turned to his mates: 'Did you hear that? I started it and everyone followed.' It made his day, probably his year too. 'Goodnight Irene', incidentally, was adopted by Rovers fans in the 1950s so it's another one that's been around longer than nearly all the supporters.

It was just before he composed the rather more famous 'Pomp and Circumstance' that Sir Edward Elgar wrote a song in honour of Wolves striker Billy Malpass after seeing him play in 1898. Strangely, 'He Banged the Leather for Goal' never really caught on.

Football was clearly important to singer/songwriter Kirsty MacColl, who died tragically young at the age of 41 in a diving accident when she was hit by a powerboat. Her songs were often bitter about men and in one she wrote, 'He looked into my eyes, just as an airplane roared above. Said something about football, but he never mentioned love.' In another, where a woman finds out the truth about a man she's watching football with in a pub: 'You lied about your status, you lied about your life. You forgot you had three children, you forgot you had a wife. Now it's England 2 Colombia 0 and I know just how those Colombians feel. It's not in my nature to ever pick the winning team.' Beyond sad in so many ways.

It was an Adele of an FA Cup run* for non-league Chorley in the much-interrupted 2020/21 season as the players celebrated each and every win with a lusty rendition of Adele's 'Someone Like You'. The singer herself approved the choice with a heart emoji on Twitter. Of course, the fans joined in – but only from their sofas as the fourth-round climax of the club's great run was played out in lockdown and they weren't allowed near the Lancashire ground. In fact, a video of the players singing along in the dressing room after a previous win attracted some criticism as they were clearly forgetting to socially distance in the excitement of the moment. A bit of a storm in a teacup in as much as they hadn't been distanced out on the pitch for the previous 90 minutes either. Manager Jamie Vermiglio said, 'When you've got people stuck at home and not able to see their families, and they see a group of 20 players singing, we absolutely understand that does not look good. We've learnt from it and will set a really good example next time and do it in a bit more of a socially distant manner that's readily accepted in the eyes of the public and the laws and legislations that are there at the moment.' * Adele pun courtesy of *The Sun*.

Lots of football clubs have – or perhaps had – special songs associated with their fans: 'Keep Right on to the End of the Road' (Birmingham); 'Delilah' (Stoke); '1-0 to the Arsenal' (well, the Gunners, of course); 'Blaydon Races' (Newcastle); 'When the Saints Go Marching In' (Southampton); 'Play Up Pompey' (Portsmouth); 'Hi Ho Wolverhampton' (Wolves); 'Can't Help Falling in Love' (Sunderland); 'Glory, Glory Tottenham Hotspur' (Spurs); 'Sussex by the Sea' (Brighton); 'Greasy Chip Butty' (Sheffield United); 'Sailing' (Chesterfield); 'Let 'Em All Come Down to The Den' or 'No One Likes Us' (Millwall).

The England national team have had various songs written about them over the years to boost them in major tournaments, though the jury's well and truly out on whether they make a blind bit of difference. They include, and feel free to choose your own favourite from this list,

'World Cup Willie' (Lonnie Donegan), 'Back Home' (England's 1970 World Cup squad), 'World in Motion' (New Order), 'Three Lions' (Skinner, Baddiel and The Lightning Seeds), 'Vindaloo' (Fat Les).

And there's probably a whole book to be written about chants or songs that fans have made up. Some of the occasionally very clever lines to enjoy are:

'We've got Di Canio, You've got our stereos' – West Ham fans to Liverpool.

'He's fast, he's red, he talks like Father Ted, Robbie Keane' – Liverpool chant about Dublin-born striker Keane.

'Dicks out! Dicks out!' – Fulham fans' tongue-in-cheek provocation about unpopular manager Alan Dicks.

'And all the runs that Kinky makes are blinding' – Manchester City fans about Georgi Kinkladze.

'He's big, he's red, his feet stick out of bed' – Liverpool fans greet their new signing, Peter Crouch.

'He scores goals, my lord, he scores goals' – Manchester United fans eulogise Paul Scholes.

'Stayed in a burger, you should have stayed in a burger' – Crystal Palace fans to Colchester keeper Dean Gerken.

'His name's a department store, you know he's gonna score' – Bury fans sing about John Lewis.

'We've got Fabrizio, you've got fuck-allio' – Derby fans serenade Fabrizio Ravenelli.

'That vegan bastard, he's eating our grass' – Walsall fans to an injured Forest Green player.

'He's Brazilian, he only cost 50 million, and we think he's fucking brilliant' – Everton fans to Richarlison.

'He's one of our own' – Spurs pride in home-grown Harry Kane.

'Rafa's got his Dirk Kuyt' – witty Liverpool support for Rafa Benitez signing.

'Sold to the USA' – Manchester United fans are teased about the club being taken over in 2005.

'You're not incredible' – Manchester City fans single out Porto's Hulk.

'Blobby for England' – Chelsea fans after Barnet's comfortably sized player/manager/goalkeeper Gary Phillips had made some good saves against them.

'Here's to you, Danny Drinkwater, Leicester loves you more than you will know' – on the way to the 2016 Premier League title.

'When you're sat in row Z and the ball hits your head, that's Zamora' – Fulham fans on Bobby Zamora.

'He's got red hair but we don't care' – Everton fans to manager David Moyes.

'There's only one F in Tardif' – Guernsey fans honour long-serving goalkeeper Chris Tardif. Usually followed by fans tittering behind their hands and looking embarrassed at how bold they've been.

'You'll never beat Des Walker' – Nottingham Forest fans serenading their legendary defender.

'Where were you when you were us?' – AFC Wimbledon fans to MK Dons.

'You're just a shit Chas & Dave' – Spurs fans to Manchester City supporters Noel and Liam Gallagher.

'You only live round the corner' – Fulham fans to Manchester United supporters.

'Deep fry yer pizzas, we're gonna deep fry yer pizzas' – Scotland fans at a World Cup match trying to hurt Italian feelings.

'We've got Novak, our carpets are filthy' – Huddersfield fans to Lee Novak.

A classic pun to finish with there. And then there's these old chestnuts which can be (and are) sung anywhere:

'I predict a diet' – to any opposition player who's carrying even a tiny bit of spare timber. Also 'Who ate all the pies' in the same situation.

'Is this is a library?' – if the opposition fans aren't singing; see also 'You're not singing any more' and 'It's all gone quiet over there'.

'We can see you sneaking out' – when any opposition fan is spotted going to the toilet.

'Four-three, we're gonna win four-three' – compulsory to sing whenever your team goes 3-0 down.

'One-nil to the referee' – if your team has fallen behind to a disputed penalty; 'You should have gone to Specsavers' – any controversial decision by officials.

'Let's all have a disco' – party time if your team is in a position where it's impossible to lose; 'This is the best trip I've ever been on' – away fans anywhere when they're winning.

'Staying up, staying up, staying up' – whenever a team threatened with relegation look like they're going to get a point.

'He's here, he's there, he's every-fucking-where' – sang in honour of the team's busiest midfielder. But if the player's name is added it's got to have just three syllables, like Alan

Ball or Mason Mount, to make it scan. Same goes for 'He gets the ball, he does fuck-all'.

'You dirty northern bastards' – works the other way, too, with southern in for northern.

'You thought you had scored, you were wrong' – compulsory when an opposition shot hits the side-netting and their fans mistakenly think it might have been a goal.

'Come in a taxi. Did you come in a taxi?' – when the away fans are few and far between.

'Come back when your balls have dropped' – if some of the opposition singers sound a bit on the young side.

'You're supposed to be at home' – taunt by away fans if they're outsinging the opposition.

'What's it like to see a crowd?' (same as the last one).

'We're gonna score one more than you' – self-explanatory.

'Two-four-six-eight, who do we appreciate?' – think that one died out about the time colour TV was invented.

'Ten men, we only need ten men' – on those rare occasions when a team have had a player sent off but are still winning.

'My garden shed is bigger than this' – away fans' taunt about the size of the home stand.

'Que sera, sera, whatever will be, we're going to Wemberley' – special song for cup tie victories, whatever the round, with a suitable mispronunciation for rhyming purposes.

'Let's pretend we've scored a goal' – losing team's fans play make-believe.

'Shoes off if you love …' – accompanied by waving your shoes in the air.

'Stand up if you still believe' – it would be rude to keep sitting.

'It's just like watching Brazil' – when your team threads together three passes in a row.

'You're shit and you know you are' – preferably to be sung at your opponents rather than your own team; 'You're so shit it's unbelievable' – same as the previous one.

'So fucking easy, this is so easy fucking easy' – nothing like rubbing it in if you're winning; Also, 'Can we play you every week?'

'We shall not be moved' – sticking with your team.

'He scores when he wants' – bet he wishes he could.

'You're getting sacked in the morning' – taunt aimed at unpopular opposition manager (well, any opposition manager really).

'My niece of two is better than you' – happy days when an opponent shanks a shot into the roof of the stand.

There are, of course, other witty chants that can – and are – sung by fans at games throughout the football pyramid. And, of course, there's the very special 'We Are the Champions' but many fans have a lifetime of following football without ever being able to sing that one. Except to take the mickey.

And finally in a chapter which has captured the wit and imagination of musical maestros in grounds everywhere: Graham Gooch hit a century for Essex against the West Indies when the first floodlit cricket match in the country for 28 years was staged at Stamford Bridge in 1980. I can see this one coming but when Chelsea used the ground for the more traditional football the following weekend and put in a below-par performance, the fans chanted, 'We want our cricket back!'

20

Fans' lives: I did it my way

IT SOUNDS pretty entertaining now but, of course, it wasn't at all funny for poor Richard Busby's mum when she went to her first – and last – game. He said, 'My mother only ever went to one football match. My dad took her to see Blackpool when they were on holiday there. She didn't enjoy it at all as it was cold and wet and in the last few minutes, an untypically wild kick by Stanley Matthews went into the crowd and knocked off her fine new hat, ruining it. She never went again!'

When he was a boy, Ian Thompstone remembers his dad taking him into Manchester city centre on the bus and walking through Piccadilly Gardens to Market Street where there was a Kardomah café. His dad said it was where the Manchester United players would sometimes meet after training to chat and listen to music. One day father and son were walking past and there were several bicycles chained up so they knew the United players were inside. The Thompstones went in and there were many of the Busby Babes, just relaxing and enjoying themselves and integrating as part of the community. Ian recognised players like David Pegg and Eddie Colman from their pictures on football cards he collected. Tragically, both were killed in the Munich air disaster soon afterwards. A poignant memory.

Pauline Clarke grew up in London but developed a passion for Manchester United after seeing them play at Spurs in 1958. She used to get a coach from London Victoria at 10.30pm on a Friday, arriving at Manchester Piccadilly at 6am. She would help out by selling programmes outside the ground and afterwards stay at a YWCA hostel before returning home the next day. Someone told a newspaper that a 'London girl' was travelling alone to watch games at Old Trafford, which was reckoned to be pretty unusual for an 18-year-old in those days. The next thing she knew she was being introduced to United manager Sir Matt Busby, his deputy Jimmy Murphy and several players, and her story appeared in the papers and on local TV. With some friends she set up the London branch of the Manchester United Supporters' Club, but later moved north herself as she married Don, the cousin of Roger Byrne, one of the other United players killed at Munich in 1958.

It was his mum's washing powder that helped West Ham fan Steve Davies become such a committed fan. He told *The Guardian* in an interview about the day he came on as a substitute replacement for striker Lee Chapman: 'When Persil printed vouchers on the sides of their soapboxes for discounted train tickets, it made travelling support feasible for an entire generation of youngsters. Mum bought the Persil, I cut the coupons out, and I was off. I'd get stuck in places like Sheffield and couldn't get home, sleeping in empty stations. It was brilliant.'

Future England international and comedy legend Peter Crouch was just a young striker making his way in football when I saw him playing at Gillingham for Portsmouth. Whenever he went near the ball, rather too many home fans would embarrassingly shriek 'freak' – as if they'd never seen anyone over six feet tall before. I thought it happened everywhere he went, but Crouch hit back much later when he singled out Gillingham fans as hillbillies. He got stick for that, too. More confident as he got older about taking fans on, Crouch recalled one particular incident in his end-of-career book *How to Be a Footballer*. He got a tweet from @Smiggy – possibly not his real name – saying that if he scored for Stoke that day against Chelsea, the fan would get a tattoo of Crouch's arse on his face to mark his 17th birthday. Crouch reckoned his backside wouldn't look much different to anybody else's on Smiggy's face, and that he probably meant it the other way round. That he'd get a tattoo of Crouch's face on his arse. Stoke duly beat Chelsea and Crouch had the last word when he responded to Smiggy by asking him when his birthday was. Think the reply got lost in the post.

The trouble with tattoos is they're not just for Christmas. In fact, by the time the next Christmas has come round that urgent reason for getting a commemorative tattoo may well have been well forgotten. Football is ephemeral, a tattoo is forever. More or less.

For example, passionate Leeds United fan Hayden Kershaw got a tattoo done to mark the achievement of

Marco Bielsa in transforming his beloved team. Then again, Don Revie was a pretty good manager for Leeds back in the day, and one day someone else will have taken over the hot seat from the much-loved Bielsa. But the tat will still be there large as life on Hayden's left leg.

And just to prove the point without labouring it, a Birmingham City fan got the face of manager Gary Monk tattooed on his backside after the club avoided relegation in 2019. And where is Monk now? Well, what a bummer – he's no longer in charge of Birmingham.

At least N'Golo Kante's face is a little higher up than the backside of French non-league footballer Alain Bulteel. He got a tattoo of the midfielder's smiling face on his lower back after losing a bet with mates who said France would win the 2018 World Cup. 'When you lose a bet you have to take the consequences,' said Alain, making his forever commitment to the Kante tattoo.

The expression 'Cantona's got your back' is absolutely true for Manchester United fan Jamie Wright. He's got a giant tattoo of a painting called *The Art of the Game* by Manchester artist Michael Browne, which is on show in the National Football Museum. The picture draws a parallel between a 15th century painting of the Resurrection and Cantona's return to football after his eight-month ban for his famous kung-fu assault on a Crystal Palace fan. Jamie said, 'Eric is an icon and this is something I've thought about getting for years and years. He's given his approval for the tattoo and that meant a lot.'

Tattoo artists in Manchester were also kept pretty busy commemorating that incredible moment when

Sergio Agüero scored the dramatic last-minute winning goal against QPR to clinch the 2011/12 Premier League championship. But surely there's only just the one man walking around with a tattoo on his arm of Martin Tyler's Sky commentary description of that legendary moment. I wonder if he often shows it off down the pub when he's had an armful.

It made his day for an Everton fan when he offered James Rodríguez a bottle of Echo Falls wine, and the recently acquired Colombian international opened his car window on the way out from the training ground and graciously accepted the gift. The fan didn't get a selfie as he was too excited at the time, so he went out and got a tattoo of the moving moment. Now he can be reminded forever of the day a player took his bottle.

Newcastle fan Robert Nesbitt got his timing all wrong when he decided to get a tattoo of his favourite player, Andy Cole, on his thigh. It wasn't long after the ink dried that Cole upped and joined Manchester United. No probs for Rob as he reverted to plan B, and turned the tattoo into a tribute to Les Ferdinand instead.

Many fans have tattoos of favourite players' faces – those featured include David Beckham, Alan Shearer, Jamie Carragher, his mate Gary Neville, John Terry and Frank Lampard (these two together on the same admittedly rather large stomach of a Chelsea fan), Kolo Touré (though the surname was spelled wrongly in that particular tattoo) and Diego Maradona (on some poor fan's head). Sorry to say but some looked no more like the player in question than that notorious statue of Cristiano Ronaldo at Madeira airport.

Staying with airports, Wolves supporter Steve Horton couldn't believe it would cost more than £100 for a return train journey to watch his team play at Newcastle in December 2018. So he flew there instead. Via Spain. Steve went from Birmingham to Alicante with Ryanair and then came straight back to Newcastle from the Costa Brava, for a combined fare of less than a ton. Wolves away to Newcastle, it's all good as long as you remember to take your passport.

There's a joker in every group of long-suffering fans and Tim Jones is the man at Wrexham. He turned up at Liverpool's John Lennon airport for an away trip with the guys carrying a giant 5ft boarding pass. Apparently there were no rules regarding the size of passes and he had to be allowed on the Ryanair flight to Algarve. It was only a series of pre-season friendlies that the Wrexham fans were off to watch but Tim brightened their day with what they called his 'hilarious prank'. That Tim, eh, always up for a laugh.

It was a hell of a journey from Australia to Kiev to watch the 2018 Champions League Final. But it must have seemed even further going back again afterwards for Liverpool fan Matteo Siano. Back home, his parents had bought him a £1,950 trip to the Ukraine for a surprise 21st birthday present. It involved five countries, with three flights, a train journey, and 14 hours on a coach. Matteo, who was studying at university in Brisbane at the time, jumped at the chance but suffered the disappointment of seeing his team lose 3-1 to Real Madrid.

And while we're in Australia, I loved the tale of the rugby fan (it's not football but it's a good story) who set his heart on seeing the 2015 Rugby World Cup Final. Trouble is it was at Twickenham and he was on the other side of the world. No problem. He took the Friday off work, flew across the world to arrive 24 hours later in London just in time to see the match, and then flew straight back after. Can you imagine him going into the office on the Monday morning and being asked if he'd had a good weekend? 'Yes, thanks, but we lost the match.' Expect he fell asleep at his desk soon after.

Fans who love a good trip to an away game have quite a bond with motorways considering the time they spend together – Ali King told of travelling eight hours on a coach from Yeovil Town to watch his team play at Carlisle. One year it was straight after watching Yeovil at Middlesbrough the previous Tuesday, so the supporters had spent 32 hours together in travelling time over five days. That's quite a few cans of beer and hands of cards at the back of the bus.

And what about those motorway service station breaks? Dave Sinfield posted on Facebook about how he and his Maidstone United-supporting mates took a football with them on the coach to away matches and always set up a game in the car park. Better still if fans on the way to games elsewhere turned up and they would play against them. He remembered losing heavily to West Ham fans who had a convoy of six coaches of supporters to pick a team from, having a hard-fought draw with Stoke, and putting loads of goals past a hungover Gillingham keeper in a service station Kent derby. And he recalled a massive snowball fight with Brentford one cold January day on

FANS' LIVES: I DID IT MY WAY

the way to their respective matches. Much better snowball fights with rival fans than real ones.

Staying with bad weather, it was very disappointing for Burton Albion fans when they arrived in Bournemouth in 2014 for an FA Cup tie only for the match to be postponed. Kind home supporters clubbed together and raised £3,000 to cover their expenses. Burton paid their coach fares with the money and the rest went to charity.

Others have told of travelling huge distances only for a match to be postponed – Derek Richardson drove from Newcastle to Plymouth for a Monday night game only for it to be called off. And anyway, it was due to be televised live!

I can remember being on the M4 on my way to a match one Saturday lunchtime and seeing a coach coming the other way carrying the team I was going to watch. In a bizarre moment, I thought they'd lost their way, but we made the sensible decision to stop at the next services (no mobiles in those days) to ring the ground. We found out the match had been called off at midday and the team were heading back home. We turned round and went to watch Brentford play instead, so that was a bonus.

Talking of wasted journeys, Sunderland fans trekked down to seven Wembley finals in all the years after they famously won the FA Cup in 1973, and each time they saw their team lose. So it was sod's law that when the club finally broke that hoodoo and beat Tranmere 1-0 to win the EFL Trophy at Wembley in March 2021 none of them were allowed to go because of coronavirus.

It's such a preposterous story it must be true but Luke Piper – and his unlucky mate – have vivid memories of travelling to Chester by coach to watch their team, Darlington. He told the story on Facebook of how they were messing about after arriving at 11am in plenty of time for kick-off. One lad jumped on another one's back, and the man underneath fell flat on his face, shattering his kneecap. He refused to go to hospital, opting to go to the pub and then the match, as planned. Outside the stadium before the game, the pain and booze combined powerfully and he passed out. He was taken to hospital, accompanied by loyal Luke, and later the pair discovered they'd missed the coach home and, even worse, their team had lost 3-0. With his mate in a cast and hobbling on crutches, and the last train also already gone, they were stuck. So they politely asked Luke's girlfriend and her 'pregnant friend' – love that bit of detail – to make the 300-mile round trip from Darlington to drive them home, arriving back in the early hours of Sunday morning.

Even an injury-time winning goal by Harry Kane which secured England a place in the World Cup finals couldn't lift the mood of the Wembley crowd after a 1-0 defeat of Slovenia in a qualifying group game in October 2017. It was a disappointing match and a poor England performance, and manager Gareth Southgate admitted afterwards that he became aware of the crowd's discontent in the second half. The normally passionate and loyal fans turned to amusing themselves by throwing paper aeroplanes at each other. Neil Thompstone, who was there with his young son Noah, remembered: 'The game was crap, really dour, and the best moment of the night came when one of the paper aeroplanes was thrown from the top tier at Wembley and managed to "score" in Joe Hart's net right in front of us! Huge cheer. It was a great moment.'

Northern Ireland fan Jay Keating performed CPR on an elderly man who had collapsed near the Stade de France before his country's match against Sweden in Euro 2016, but then realised he'd lost his ticket to the game. Four fellow fans felt so sorry for the Good Samaritan that they clubbed together to buy him a replacement. One of them, Brian Kerrigan, told the *Irish Mirror*, 'He was the real hero, what he did was a much bigger deal than what we did.'

My own family has a long football-following tradition, and when asked what he would like for a treat after a stay in hospital, my then teenage son didn't hesitate: 'To see a football match in Italy.' Good lad, I thought, I can arrange that. And, of course, I'd have to go with him because he wasn't old enough to do it alone.

We went to Genoa and visited Sampdoria's training ground where Roberto Mancini signed his autograph book. We then caught a train to Milan and watched an AC Milan match at the San Siro, followed by Turin where we saw Torino play a Lazio side containing Paul Gascoigne. And the following night we went back to the same stadium to watch Juventus play Paris Saint-Germain in a UEFA Cup semi-final.

We bought numbered tickets for seats in the stand that night but couldn't quite work out how the system worked and where we should be sitting. My Italian is non-existent but I gathered from a steward that it was first-come first-served and we could sit where we liked in that particular section. So we grabbed front-row seats and I could see what the steward meant as gradually our row filled up, then the one behind, and so on. Five minutes from the start everybody along from us stood up to let two men come bustling through. As luck would have it, the two seats we'd taken were actually theirs, and they insisted on us moving.

There was nothing I could do about it, so we looked behind and the whole section was virtually full by now and only the odd back-row seat available for us. But a nearby couple got up and insisted we took their place instead. We picked out two words from what they were saying as an explanation for their kindness. One was 'English' and the other 'bambino'. I've assumed to this day they were trying to say they wanted an English family to appreciate that Italians were kind and hospitable, and my son – hardly a bambino at 15 – was only a child and warranted a front-row seat. Have you ever tried to sincerely thank someone in a language you can't speak?

21

Literature and arts:
Is this is a library?

AT THE time of writing, almost a century had passed since Nottingham Forest fan and novelist J.B. Priestley wrote one of his best-known books, *The Good Companions*. It's certainly a sentence and a half but the following quote shows how being a football fan hasn't really altered much over all those years in between: 'Paying your shilling at the turnstile turned you into a member of a new community, all brothers together for an hour and a half, for not only had you escaped from the clanking machinery of this lesser life, from work, wages, rent, doles, sick pay, insurance cards, nagging wives, ailing children, bad bosses, idle workmen, but you had escaped with most of your mates and your neighbours, with half the town, and there you were, cheering together, thumping one another on the shoulders, swopping judgements like lords of the earth, having pushed your way through a turnstile into another and altogether more splendid kind of life, hurtling with conflict and yet passionate and beautiful in its art. Moreover it offered you more than a shilling's worth of material for talk during the rest of the week. A man who had missed the last home match had to enter social life on tiptoe in Bruddersford.'

I found the extract astonishing. Not just because it took me so long to read as I don't ever remember coping with a sentence containing 117 words before, but also because of the picture painted by Priestley. I'd assumed that camaraderie and commitment were qualities that fans had gradually taken on board during the second half of the 20th century. Before that, I thought spectators patiently queued to take their place standing on the terraces, lit a fag or two, and did nothing else except politely applaud at the end of each half. And perhaps rattle their rattles and wave the scarves their wives had knitted them for Christmas.

TV writer and producer Charlie Brooker put it better than me: 'Back in the 1930s when men with handlebar moustaches played football in long johns and tails, did fans weep in the stand when their team lost? No. They limited their responses to a muttered "blast" or muted "hurrah" before going home to smoke a pipe and lean on the mantelpiece.'

French writer (and goalkeeper!) Albert Camus added to our knowledge of what draws us all to football with his own take on the game he loved. 'Everything I know about morality and the obligations of men, I owe it to football,' he said. He was a philosopher so he understood more about these things than most of us. But what he meant was that the simplistic morality of football contradicted the complicated morality imposed by the state and the

Church. This, of course, was a view expressed in the mid-20th century and perhaps football can't boast exactly the same simplistic morality today.

What Camus also loved about football was the team spirit, the brotherhood and the common purpose of the 11 players taking to the field together. He kept goal for the Racing Universitaire d'Alger team in Algeria in the late 1920s and won praise for his enthusiasm and courage. But tuberculosis ended his promising football career, although he continued to love the game and learn lessons from it.

Even the mighty William Shakespeare got in on the football act, mentioning it in *King Lear* when the Earl of Kent taunts a servant with the accusation that he's just a 'base football player'.

No evidence exists of the famous author of the best-selling series of books in history watching West Ham, incognito or not. It's a story that's been bandied about, but what is definite is that the club get a mention in JK Rowling's *Harry Potter* blockbusters. West Ham is the only Muggle football team to be named and it's said to be in honour of a friend of Rowling's called Troy, who's a dedicated Hammers fan. In three of the books in the series, half-wizard Dean Thomas has a poster of the team above his bed at Hogwarts School of Witchcraft and Wizardry. It always bemused fellow pupil Ron Weasley, who didn't understand the appeal of football. In the Danish version of one of the books, West Ham are somewhat mysteriously replaced by Liverpool. Rowling herself has indicated she's not much of a football follower but her dad supported Spurs so that would be her team, too.

Novelist Martin Amis loves football but hated hooliganism and nationalistic tribal feelings. He wrote in *The Observer* about his favourites, Manchester United, winning the Champions League in 1999 and talked about 'the fabulous lurch of emotion' brought about by the last few minutes of the game. He concluded, 'Stranger turned to stranger with love and triumph. All were lost in the great red sea.'

Clockwork Orange author Anthony Burgess had a character state in one of his books, 'Today is Saturday. Five days shalt thou labour, as the Bible says. The seventh day is the Lord thy God's. The sixth day is for football.' Apparently Burgess was interested in football but said in his autobiography he'd only ever attended one match, at Manchester City in 1928, which he remembered for the passion and the obscenities. In an article in *Time* magazine he reflected, 'Soccer is traditionally crude, and attracts roughs, drunks and roarers. It cannot be discussed in pubs without passion and obscenity. It is certainly not a gentleman's game.'

The poet Philip Larkin compares supporters at Aston Villa with a moving image of innocent-looking men who had just signed up to fight in the war. In his poem about the First World War, *MCMXIV*, he wrote, 'Those long uneven lines, standing as patiently, as if they were stretched outside, The Oval or Villa Park.'

Roughly 500 years ago, an anonymous Scottish poet wrote – tongue in cheek – about the game in a poem entitled *The Beauties of Foot-ball*. Translated into modern English it will resonate with many a retired footballer:

'Bruised muscles and broken bones, strife, discord, and futile blows, kamed in old age, then crippled withal, these are the beauties of football.'

Sir Arthur Conan Doyle was a keen sportsman when he wasn't writing Sherlock Holmes books and was a goalkeeper for an amateur side in Portsmouth, playing under the pseudonym A.C. Smith. He also took the wicket of W.G. Grace while playing cricket. Okay, that's not football, but we'd all dine out on that moment for the rest of our life, wouldn't we?

And in this chapter on the heady mixture of arts and football, the Gallagher brothers might dispute this, but the most famous Manchester City fan of all time was a gentleman who died in 1976 at the age of 88. L.S. Lowry's work lives on though, and two paintings which demonstrate his love of football have both subsequently sold for millions. *Going to the Match*, showing fans entering Bolton's old ground Burnden Park, was bought for £1.9m by the Professional Footballers' Association in 1999 at Sotheby's in London. A second work, *The Football Match*, which hadn't been seen in public for many years, was sold for £5,641,250 at Christie's in London in May 2011.

The painting had been in a private collection since soon after it was finished in 1949 and was described by Christie's as 'a modern masterpiece'. The work depicts hundreds of Lowry's famous stick figures at a football match, against a backdrop of factories with billowing chimneys. Philip Harley of Christie's said it was the ultimate example of the artist's work – and of football. He said, 'The large format, panoramic, bird's-eye composite view of Lowry's own landscape perfectly captures the spirit and drama of a town gripped by the excitement of the Saturday football match.'

A bit Lowry-like, *Playing Fields* is an evocative picture of deserted football pitches set against a heavily industrialised background. It's by Eric Satchwell and can be seen in the Manchester Art Gallery. But possibly the earliest ever painting of a football match was the depiction of a game between Sunderland and Aston Villa in January 1895 by a local artist called Thomas Marie Madawaska Hemy. It was commissioned to celebrate Sunderland winning the First Division title and is on display at the club's Stadium of Light. It's been called both *The Corner Kick* and *The Last Minute – Now or Never* and carries a plaque saying it was presented to the club on 4 September 1930 by Samuel Wilson.

22

Clubs: Keep right on to the end of the road

Accrington Stanley

Out of the Football League for 44 years, Accrington Stanley were highlighted for national recognition in 1989 when the club was mentioned in a high-profile TV advert for milk. Two young Liverpool fans featured and one claimed Ian Rush said if he didn't drink lots of milk he'd only be good enough to play for Accrington Stanley. His mate replied, 'Accrington Stanley, who are they?' which became a self-deprecating club catchphrase. Stanley returned to the Football League in 2007 after that 44-year absence.

Arsenal

There's reckoned to be 27 million Arsenal fans around the world, the third-biggest global fanbase, according to a 2005 report. Yet, in the stadium itself, supporters have a reputation for being hard to please. Herbert Chapman led them to unprecedented success in the 1930s, winning the First Division and the FA Cup, but complained about the club's 'boo-boys' and also endured taunts of 'lucky Arsenal' and 'boring Arsenal'. Later, it was George Graham's turn to face criticism from fans for his tactics despite success domestically and in Europe. And, of course, Arsène Wenger's long and mainly triumphant reign ended in controversy with some fans vociferously complaining he'd outstayed his welcome.

Aston Villa

The then Duke of York, later King George VI, officially opened Aston Villa's main stand in January 1924 and said he had no idea a ground existed that was so 'finely equipped in every way – and devoted to football'. Incidentally, Villa's magnificent Holte End became the largest single-end stand in Britain when it was built.

Aston Villa were the first Premier League club to give up commercial shirt sponsorship when for two years from 2008 they wore shirts bearing the name of Acorns Children's Hospice. Following that, the hospice became the club's official charity partner.

Barnsley

A lovely moment on YouTube demonstrates what innocent fun you can have at a football match with a plant pot. For some reason, a Barnsley fan had brought one along and his mates amused themselves by taking it in turns to wear it while singing, 'He's got a plant pot on his head.' Then the wearer would whip it off and without looking throw it to another part of the crowd. Whoever caught it had to put the pot on his head so everyone could join in and point,

'He's got a plant pot on his head.' And, well, you get the idea – and so on, round the ground. One of those stories that's funnier to watch than read about!

Blackpool

What Blackpool's fans lacked in numbers compared with the other clubs in the Premier League, during their one season there in 2010/11, they made up for with noise. They were officially clocked at 85 decibels, the fifth-highest in the division. When they'd won promotion, an estimated 100,000 people lined the Golden Mile to watch an open-top bus parade, and manager Ian Holloway called it the most unbelievable moment of his life. A predecessor in his hot seat, Steve McMahon, said, 'The supporters have been fantastic and while there's that support the club can go a long way.' Unfortunately for the Blackpool fans they did go a long way, from the Premier League to the lowest tier of the Football League in five years.

Bolton Wanderers

Ups and downs are a fact of life for Bolton fans, and the club have played in all four divisions on both their old ground, Burnden Park, and its successor since 1997, now called the University of Bolton Stadium.

Bolton allegedly got their long-standing nickname of the Trotters because their fans were well known for enjoying a practical joke, known locally as trotting. It's nothing to do with pigs' trotters – or Del Boy in *Only Fools and Horses.*

Brentford

Saying goodbye is important and it was the one thing Brentford fans couldn't do when the club left their much-loved Griffin Park ground in 2020. It had been home for a massive 116 years but it went quietly into the night when no fans were allowed in for the final games there because of the coronavirus pandemic. Still, there was the new Brentford Community Stadium for fans to look forward to, but that was prohibited, too, when the following season started under lockdown and it was empty stands only.

Cambridge United

Nick Hornby is a fantastic writer and *Fever Pitch* is one of the best football books ever, but he was a bit harsh on his visit to Cambridge United: 'Cambridge had a tiny, ramshackle little ground, the Abbey Stadium (their equivalent of the Clock End was the Allotments End, and, occasionally, naughty visiting fans would nip round the back of it and hurl pensioners' cabbages over the wall), less than 4,000 watching games, and no history at all.'

Carlisle United

How happy was Laura Barr to be back on Carlisle's ground when fans were allowed to return during a break between lockdowns at the end of 2020. She tweeted a picture of the home crowd applauding as the players entered the field with the caption, 'Well, isn't this the best sight and sound. I feel I'm one of the lucky ones tonight.'

Charlton Athletic

Charlton moved to The Valley more than 100 years ago but fans had to travel to Crystal Palace or West Ham for home games for seven years when the ground was closed in 1985 for financial and safety reasons. Supporters fought a fantastic campaign to get back to The Valley and were rewarded with a place on the club's board of directors. One of the campaigners, Rick Everitt, wrote in the *Voice of the Valley* fanzine, 'It was just a football club leaving its ground, but to many, many people it was so much more. For the older fans it was the destruction of something that had run like a thread through their lives and for others it was the crushing of a dream. Charlton's moonlight flit was a cruel human tragedy.'

Fulham

Spot Hugh Grant and Richard Osman in the celebrity Craven Cottage crowd – it always seems a pleasant and serene place, somewhere nice perhaps to take your children for their first game. Fulham topped the chart in a YouGov poll to discover the best supporters in London. It would be impolite to reveal who came bottom but the lion on their badge is a clue.

For Annie Lee, Fulham brings back lovely memories: 'I worked around the corner from the Fulham ground when I was about 17, back in 1956! We young girls used to sit on a wall with our sandwiches, and watch the players train. A few romances happened, but I can't remember who the players were!' Just as well, probably, Annie.

For many fans the walk through the park alongside the Thames to the ground is one of their main memories of visiting the Cottage. Gemma Constable said, 'I always enjoyed going there, stopping off for lunch and a coffee, and strolling through the park – though it seemed a bit of a trek. Dad always said how miserable that long walk back is on a losing day!'

Forest Green Rovers
Fans of a club in a lovely part of Gloucestershire can take pride in the fact that they support world leaders in their field. Forest Green were the first vegan football club anywhere, and owners Dale Vince and Héctor Bellerín put their environmental credentials where their mouths are, insisting the players eat only meat-free products, the pitch is treated with organic fertiliser, and the whole club is carbon neutral.

Leeds United
Not only do Leeds have their own specially written song; not only do they have what the one-and-only Sir Alex Ferguson called 'probably the most intimidating ground in Europe'; not only are they consistently rated among the noisiest supporters in the land at away matches; but they also have their own salute. It's done with one arm horizontally across the chest and the fist clenched by the heart. Players have done it and fans love to do it, especially as a signal to each other in cars or coaches on the way to games, or as a greeting when they first meet. Fan Neil Jeffries explained, 'It's a wordless symbol of faith often exchanged with a total stranger.'

Manchester City

One of the country's best-supported clubs – one of the world's best come to that – Manchester City still averaged more than 30,000 fans at home matches when they were relegated to the third tier of English football in the late 1990s. Incidentally they were only the second European trophy winners to have dropped to their country's third tier, after Magdeburg in Germany. That's the same Magdeburg whose fans turned up at the ground with large fluorescent arrows and set them up pointing at the goal in an 'amusing' bid to end their team's five-game goal drought.

City fans were famous for a time for introducing the 'Poznań' celebration to English football. It involves fans turning their back on the pitch, linking arms and jumping up and down, and was started in Poland as a protest against club management, while still supporting the team. City fans dropped it after a little while when fans of other clubs mocked them by doing it if their team scored against them.

Manchester United

Former Manchester United manager Tommy Docherty, in his book *Call the Doc*, said, 'Old Trafford is the only stadium in the world I've ever been in that's absolutely buzzing with atmosphere when it's empty and there isn't a soul inside. It's almost like a cathedral.'

One of his successors, Sir Alex Ferguson, said, 'I remember in Rotterdam in 1991 for the final of the Cup Winners' Cup a lot of fans were at the main entrance chanting the names of players like "Hughesy" as they went in. Suddenly Sir Matt Busby arrived and the wild cheering turned to polite applause. It was quite touching, like the Pope arriving.'

Millwall
Millwall fan and radio presenter Danny Baker came up with a lovely quote about Brian Rioch taking over as the club's manager. 'When he came we were depressed and miserable,' said Danny. 'He's done a brilliant job of turning it around. Now we're miserable and depressed.' Baker also tells an unlikely sounding story about a park game he was playing in many years ago when the ball sailed through the serving hatch of a passing ice cream van and set off 'Greensleeves' over its loudspeaker. And yet another Baker story: As an eight-year-old, he spent ages decorating his rattle and painting it blue and white only for his dad to point out that he'd inscribed 'Up the Loins'.

Newcastle United
The late Glenn Roeder, who managed Newcastle and spent six of the best years of his playing career there, was a long way from his London roots when he first moved north. Shortly after taking over as manager in 2006, the *Daily Mail* reported his comments: 'We realised how friendly Geordies were when we lived here previously. If your car didn't start in the morning, three or four neighbours would come out and help you. In London they would come out and say "bad luck" and get in their car and drive off!'

Norwich City

We wanted to make our absent fans happy – that was the main motivation behind Norwich's quick promotion back to the Premier League in 2020/21, according to manager Daniel Farke. He said, 'We dedicate promotion to our fans because it's been such a difficult season for them. They've been fearing for their future, and for their health and that of family members and friends. It was a tough time but we hope we were able to bring them some joy, fun and distraction.'

Notts County

Fans of County have one of the best football songs – as it has nothing to do with football. Sung to the tune of 'Old Smokey', it goes, 'I had a wheelbarrow, the wheel fell off, I had a wheelbarrow, the wheel fell off, County, County, County.' Its origins are covered in the mists of time and it doesn't take itself too seriously, but it ends with a nice rousing bit for all the fans to join in.

Peterborough United

Popular Peterborough manager Chris Turner led a fans' march to the town hall to get plans approved for a new stand in 1990 in the face of opposition from local residents. Bet they loved him for that, and enjoyed his humour as well when he said before a League Cup tie, 'I've told the players we need to win so that I can have the cash to buy some new ones!'

The club's nickname, 'Posh', dates back a century to 1921 when a manager of a forerunner of the present

Peterborough United club said he was looking for 'posh players for a posh new team'. Rather surprising then, that 81 years later Victoria Beckham filed a claim with the Patent Office saying the name Posh had become synonymous with her worldwide. Her request to patent it for herself was denied.

Portsmouth

Portsmouth became the first Premier League club to go into administration, back in 2010, owing more than £100m. Fans launched a fundraising initiative to at least pay the money that was owed at the time to first aiders St John Ambulance, and enough was raised in a day to settle that debt. In 2013 the fan-owned Pompey Supporters' Trust bought out the club to save it from going into liquidation.

Sunderland

An eight-part TV documentary – the kind that's known as 'warts and all' – catalogued life behind the scenes at Sunderland Football Club during the 2017/18 season. Fans would have liked the title of the Netflix programme, *Sunderland 'Til I Die*, but not so much the content as the team ended up getting relegated.

A Sunderland season ticket holder I knew bought a ticket for an England under-21 match being staged at the Stadium of Light, even though he had no intention of going because he was working in London. It was just that he didn't want anyone else sitting in his seat.

Tranmere Rovers

Satirical rock band Half Man Half Biscuit turned down a playing appearance on the Channel 4 show *The Tube* because Tranmere were at home to Scunthorpe that evening. Lead singer and guitarist Nigel Blackwell is a big Tranmere fan (and former football fanzine editor) and even the offer of a helicopter ride back from the studio to watch the match wasn't enough.

Walsall

A witty fan came up with a nice line in toilet humour when Birmingham paper the *Sports Argus* reported Walsall needed a name for their new stadium. As it was built on the site of an old sewage works he thought it could be called WC Fields. Boom, boom. Instead, they named it the Bescot Stadium after the area where it was built, and it was later renamed Banks's Stadium.

Wigan Athletic

What a lovely idea when Wigan Athletic consulted more than 90 local primary schools to ask for ideas about what sort of mascot they should adopt for the 2019/20 season. Well done the kids, because more than half of the entries made exactly the same choice: A pie! So Crusty the Pie was the mascot of choice.

Wolverhampton Wanderers

Star Wars actor Mark Hamill is a dedicated Wolves fan – but only by accident. Asked on Twitter if he liked Wolves, Hamill thought he was being asked about animals and said yes. When it was explained to him what he'd committed to, the man who plays Luke Skywalker said, 'Everyone got so excited I had to be a fan – there's no turning back now! I'd never heard of them until two days ago but they made me feel like family.' The club commented, 'He's a good judge. The force is certainly strong at Molineux at the moment and there's an open invitation for Mark to attend a match here should his Landspeeder ever be passing.'

23

Internationals: 30
40, 50 years of hurt

THERE'S A gently sloping hill full of gift shops and local souvenirs leading up to a massive church overlooking the Adriatic Sea. Halfway up it my wife and I spotted a little café/restaurant and we stopped for lunch – a pizza and a beer, in case you wondered. This was in Croatia and the polite young man who served us spoke impeccable English. After a bit of a chat I asked him, 'Have you ever been to England?' 'No,' he replied, 'I don't like drinking and I don't like fighting.'

Is that really what Croatians think England is like? Full of people drinking and fighting? Surely that hill outside the restaurant with tourist shops catering for mature people on their way to browse inside a church wasn't constantly packed with drunk English people having a fight? Then I remembered a woman I was once talking to in California, who said when I told her I lived near London in England, 'That's where they get a lot of fog, isn't it?' You must watch a lot of very old films to have that impression, I said. Similarly the young Croatian waiter must have seen lots of hopefully pretty dated footage of English football fans causing trouble and behaving irresponsibly.

Certainly the most recent World Cup, held in Russia in 2018, was free from that sort of thing, despite dour warnings beforehand of the trouble that might be in store. Why that happened can be found in the old adage 'fail to prepare, prepare to fail'. In this country, a joint operation between the police and the Home Office resulted in more than 1,200 potential troublemakers having to hand in their passports so they couldn't travel to the tournament. Others were put off by difficulties getting visas, the cost of travel there, and – probably most significantly – the threats of what Russia might do to anyone caught causing trouble, such as five-year jail sentences. And in Russia itself, they helped by banning known gangs of 'Ultras' from games.

What followed was a party atmosphere with fans mixing and socialising together in Moscow's Red Square. It was all in stark contrast to violent scenes at Euro 2016 where Russian hooligans were blamed for starting trouble, though England supporters had also been filmed fighting in Marseille before the countries played each other.

My son was at that Russia-England match and I was horrified to watch on television as England fans were seen running for their lives at the end. They seemed to be charged by a group of what appeared to be about 200 Russian supporters, who had set off fireworks and punched their way through a line of stewards.

For the first time since he and his sister were teenagers, I was scared to go to bed without knowing that he was safely back at his accommodation. I messaged him and then did that thing of looking at my phone every two minutes to see if he'd replied. Eventually, and well after midnight, he texted and said he was fine. He and his friends had avoided any trouble, found a quiet French bar to have a couple of winding-down drinks, and were now going to bed.

He later told me, 'You don't have to worry. In situations like that you just have to work out where it's safe to go and where it isn't. If you want to find trouble it's easy, but if you want to avoid it, then that's easy too.' I believed him, but to this very day I don't know whether I should.

Fans had been injured that night, some seriously, and the police had to use tear gas and a water cannon in the worst violence seen around football since the 1998 World Cup. Former sports minister Gerry Sutcliffe told *The Observer* that it was an embarrassing day for the country. 'I thought we had got past this, I really did,' he said.

Of course, you always tend to suspect that the thugs who caused trouble around away matches for England were just there for the thrill of the violence and the heavy drinking, not for the football itself. Perhaps that's simplistic but this has certainly been a stain on our football – and the perception of our national character, come to that – for many years.

In 1995 a friendly between the Republic of Ireland and England in Dublin was abandoned when English fans began to rip out seats and throw debris and benches. Twenty people were hurt and 40 arrested.

I was at Wembley the day in 1977 when Scottish fans invaded the pitch and pulled down the goals. When I say I was there, that's not quite true as I'd been to the match but was on my way up Wembley Way to the underground station when it all took off. I didn't find out about it until much later in the evening through the TV news, but I never minded that I'd missed that iconoclastic moment. High jinks had pretty quickly spilled over into destructive mindlessness, but at least other people weren't hurt.

And it's nice to know hooliganism wasn't a 20th-century invention. In the 14th century, football games between rival English villages were unruly and violent, and King Edward II banned matches because he believed the disorder surrounding them might lead to more trouble, or even treason. And football was banned by King Edward IV in the 15th century because he wanted every 'strong and able-bodied person' to practise shooting with a bow and arrow because the defence of the country depended on it. I don't know whether to believe this but it's said that football reappeared in the early 1800s at Newgate Prison in London. Inmates apparently came up with a game that could be played with their feet as they'd all had their hands chopped off for being found guilty of robbery.

Around the world, fear of hooliganism and disruption hasn't spoiled the passion for football for millions. Nelson Mandela was famous for his love of sport, and even on the day of his inauguration as president of South Africa in 1994 he stopped off to watch a football match. While in prison on Robben Island he said he and fellow inmates discovered that football 'made us feel alive and triumphant despite the situation we found ourselves in'.

Not only was Uruguay the first country to stage the World Cup, it also lays claim to having the world's first football fanatic. While spectators everywhere else quietly watched a match, occasionally politely applauding, Prudencio Reyes would go completely apeshit back in the early 1900s. He'd shout, cheer, jump up and down, and generally go a bit mad in a manner befitting a fan of 100 years later. His role at the club he loved, Nacional, was to prepare the kit, clean boots and blow up balls. Because of the blowing-up bit he was known as the puffer – 'el hinchador' – and the word hincha became commonplace in the Spanish language as a term for fans.

Plenty of learned research has gone into all aspects of football and what makes a fan a fan. For instance, university researchers at Reading were part of a team who studied hundreds of matches played behind closed doors throughout Europe after lockdowns started in 2020. They found what they called a 'large and statistically significant effect on the number of yellow cards issued'. This was in respect of fewer yellows being awarded to away teams, leaving open the question of whether vociferous home crowds increase the pressure on referees. They also found that, on average, home teams won 36 per cent of matches compared with 46 per cent when crowds were present.

For every fan who supports a generally successful club, such as one of the so-called big six in the Premier League, there's someone else whose team never seem to win anything. Or even have a sniff of a chance of winning anything. So why do those fans continue to show such committed support? Martha Newson, a cognitive anthropologist who was mentioned earlier for recommending soothing music at the end of matches, also researched this subject and presented some of her findings in a magazine, *The Conversation*. She concluded, 'Football fans tend to be highly loyal to their group, an intense state of belonging called identity fusion. Most fans are recruited through existing relational ties – for example, through a parent, cousin or friend. This can lead to complex and enduring networks that are hard to cut off. For long-suffering fans of poorly performing clubs the answer to the question "Why do I do put myself through this?" could well be "Because I love the club so much." This might be an attempt to reduce the dissonance of spending lots of time and money on a club that never "pays out" with victory.' She added that experiences such as relegation, or perhaps a bitter defeat in a local derby, lead to even stronger bonding with the rest of the group that cements everyone together for much longer.

Her views were echoed by Dr Sandy Wolfson, a sports psychologist at Northumbria University and a Newcastle season ticket holder. Her research into the subject showed that identifying as a member of the group is far more important to the fan than the actual outcome of the match. 'In fact it gets to the point where abandoning your team is an impossibility, because you see the team as part of your identity,' she said.

Dr Wolfson recruited volunteers through fan websites to answer questions and said her findings showed, 'When you've won, obviously you're basking in reflected glory, but when you lose you have some repair work to do and have to think creatively about how you can justify your membership of the group.' She also discovered that only when a team are neither doing well nor badly, but languishing in the middle of the table, did fans tend to be less optimistic about their club's future.

Researchers for the energy company Utilita uncovered some interesting results – and some pretty obvious ones – when they made a study of what we football fans love most. Top in their survey, which was aimed at helping clubs keep their energy costs down during times of financial hardship, was the atmosphere at a live game. This was followed by a last-minute winning goal, victory in a derby game, wonder goals, and cup upsets. Other things that fans said they loved about football included watching balls being plucked out of a velvet bag to determine cup draws, supporting the underdog, seeing rivals get relegated and the opportunity just to get out of the house. Oh, and the smell of the burger van. The research also found two-thirds of football lovers will ditch all other plans and activities on a matchday to watch their side play.

All sorts of academic research is done on football fans, and a really positive conclusion emerged from extensive work carried out by the Social Issue Research Centre. Its conclusion was, 'While there are strong rivalries between fans at local and national levels, the striking feature of the research is the high degree to which football unites people from varied backgrounds.' They also felt that being a true fan plays a positive role in the lives of millions of us. The centre's report added, 'As football fandom is socially inherited within the family, matches regularly comprise ritualised days out for all members – toddlers and grandmothers included – and the passion for football is a unifying event. And several fan clubs across Europe are now dedicated exclusively to women and they are increasingly accepted as "authentic fans", not just the wives, girlfriends or daughters of male fans.'

Women's football itself was particularly badly hit by the coronavirus lockdown because the previous year had been its best ever in England for attendances, and the dream was to build on that. League matches were attracting four times as many fans as the previous season and a new record attendance of 38,262 was set when Spurs played Arsenal at the Tottenham Hotspur Stadium.

Fans had traditionally been on the quiet side as the game grew, and it was said grounds lacked atmosphere, but the comparatively recently formed Manchester United attracted supporters who wanted to sing and beat drums, and the players appreciated their noisy backing. It soon caught on with fans at other clubs as newcomers to enjoying women's football commented that they were surprised at the standard and passion the players displayed.

The mission was to build on the growth in support and enhanced atmospheres at matches post-pandemic. That expansion worldwide was so huge that in 2019, the Women's World Cup Final attracted a TV audience of more than a billion people.

Women's football in the UK dates back further than many of us might think, and in the 1920s matches attracted crowds of up to 50,000. But the FA stepped in and banned women's games for 50 years before relenting and allowing them again.

A film built around the subject of women's football in 2002 brought attention and understanding of the fast-growing impact of the game. *Bend It Like Beckham*, starring Parminder Nagra and Keira Knightley, was inspirational and funny as well as tackling the important subject of a Sikh girl circumventing her parents' ban on her playing 'a men's game'.

Ro Jackson, a creative consultant talking about her love of women's football, said it needed personalities like US star Megan Rapinoe for more and more young women to know and love the game. She said, 'It's harder to be a fan of women's football, but there are things we can do. Click a link when a female athlete is featured, turn up to club matches, tune into broadcast matches, support a local grassroots team, ensure there are equal sport opportunities in school if you have kids. It's not easy, but these ways will help.'

Claire, who enjoys watching both men's and women's football, told the award-winning arseblog that she's grown to prefer the latter: 'There are three reasons I like women's football more than men's: 1) I like the fact that they cheat less and spend less time rolling around on the floor; 2) The players have more time for the fans and seem to be more appreciative of the support; 3) The atmosphere at the games between sets of supporters. For example, we have a very good relationship with the Manchester City supporters and have a lot of fun banter with them.'

And finally in this chapter I hesitate to repeat this tweet as I think 'football-loving Susan' may just have been tongue in cheek when she wrote, 'My boyfriend told me to choose between him and football … I'm really gonna miss him.'

24

Mascots: Always look on the bright side of life

THE GOOD news is you get in free, you get a ringside view of the match, you get to meet and greet as many fellow fans as you like, you get to high-five the players, and if you're at a big club you get paid as well. The bad news is you have to dress up and look a bit of a twat. Though come to think of it, that in itself is good news as nobody need know who's inside the costume so you retain your anonymity.

Mascots have come from nowhere to become essential in a comparatively short space of time, and more or less every top club has to have one nowadays – well, as long as there are crowds in the stadium to amuse. The idea is to increase bonding with fans, especially young ones, and make their visit to football even more of a memorable experience. And also, no surprise here, to help promote the sale of merchandise in the club shop.

But it was Arsenal who decided they could go without their famous mascot as the fan inside the Gunnersaurus costume was made redundant during the height of the panic over coronavirus in 2020/21. As a PR move it was a disaster because it came just after the club had been able to afford £45m to buy midfielder Thomas Partey. Despite being out of first team favour by then, German international Mesut Özil intervened and offered to pay for what he called 'the big green guy' all the time he was a player at the club. Özil has form for kind gestures and although he undoubtedly wasn't the first footballer ever to do it, he asked guests at his 2019 wedding to donate money to a specific charity rather than buy gifts for him and new wife Amine. Gunnersaurus, who was later reinstated, was designed in 1993 by an 11-year-old boy in a competition organised by the Junior Gunners and had been a popular part of the Arsenal scene ever since.

Mascots have been known to get involved in the odd controversy and Watford's Harry the Hornet got some stick for mocking Crystal Palace's Wilfried Zaha after the clubs had drawn 1-1 on Boxing Day 2016. Zaha had been booked for simulation during the game and as he was walking off afterwards Hornet Harry dived on the ground in front of him. Gareth Evans, the man inside Harry, told Football 365, 'The fans were calling him a diver, so I just dived on the ground. Nothing more, nothing less. But it got a reaction from the Palace fans, so I did it again – why wouldn't I?' Palace manager Sam Allardyce said it was out of order but Watford boss Walter Mazzarri played down the incident: 'Let's laugh all together about this. Everything doesn't have to be a drama.'

Seemingly as equable a manager as you would like to meet, Roy Hodgson was reminded of the incident when he took over as Palace manager and Watford were their next opponents. He said, 'If you're asking me whether Harry the Hornet, who I presume is the mascot, should dive in that way, I think it's disgraceful. But of course teams try to take every advantage they can. I would be very disappointed if the Palace mascot was doing something like that to provoke the crowd against an opponent. And if I found out about it, I would stop it.'

All Harry the Hornet did was dive a couple of times, but Swansea mascot Cyril the Swan actually decapitated a rival mascot in a half-time rumpus during a match in 2001. He and Millwall's Zampa the Lion had what they later suggested was a play fight, though it ended with Cyril pulling off Zampa's head and drop-kicking it into the crowd.

Burnley's Bertie Bee has clearly played a bit of rugby in his time as he put in a superb tackle to bring a male streaker crashing down during a pitch invasion in 2002. Bertie achieved what the stewards had been failing to do – put an end to the naked man's high jinks – and then played up the crowd by celebrating with a 'worm' dance along the touchline. He wasn't quite the hero in 2013 when Burnley were playing QPR and he was sent off for offering the assistant referee a pair of spectacles. Bertie had the last word on that one, with a picture of him looking forlorn in a mocked-up jail appearing online. Actually, his forlorn face is no different to his streaker-tackling one.

As a publicity stunt, Hartlepool put their mascot up for election as mayor in 2002. And, yes you've guessed it, he only got voted in. Despite doing no serious campaigning,

Stuart Drummond finished narrowly ahead of the Labour candidate and duly took on the mayoralty. And then he became serious, giving up his mascot role as H'Angus the Monkey, and going on to win two further terms as mayor of Hartlepool.

The Aston Villa fan who took over the job of mascot Hercules the Lion decided it wasn't much fun as he couldn't get to see the match properly from inside his costume. Mind you, he said that just after he'd been sacked in 1998 for grabbing the club's beauty queen at half-time in a match. He told BirminghamLive, 'All I was doing was pulling Miss Aston Villa around, nothing more, and having a laugh.'

Then there was Spytty the Dog, mascot of a Newport County side playing in the Southern League in 2003, who offered a helping hand when a Weymouth player got injured in a match there. Ian Ridley, then chairman of Weymouth, remembered what happened next in his book, *Floodlit Dreams*: 'Our full-back Simon Browne sustained a hamstring injury and the stretcher was called for. They were one man light so the mascot lent a hand. Or a paw. Except that he dropped the stretcher and Simon went sprawling. Fans on the website wondered later how he was and Simon went on himself to say he was fine but that the Welsh idiot who had dropped him hadn't helped. That inadvertently began a racial row so I emailed Simon to tell him it might be best if he didn't contribute to the forum again.'

Mascots used to come together once a year for an annual running race in full costume – and if you ever caught sight of it on TV it's something you've probably never forgotten. It was all for charity, so that's all right then, with up to 100 characters leaping low fences in a dash to the line for the privilege of winning the Mascot Grand National. It all got a bit messy, with a complaint that fast runners were getting drafted in disguised as the mascot having never been near a football match in their life, and the event was stopped in 2013.

You'd think with all the many thousands of words in a dictionary, someone could have come up with an alternative word for mascot. There's two of them in football – the costumed animal or such like, and the youngster who proudly leads out the team.

So what's the best birthday present you can get for a football-mad eight-year-old? It has to be the chance to be the second sort of mascot for their favourite team. It's moved on a bit in the last few years but for ages it meant three things:

- Lurking outside the dressing room and then walking solemnly out alongside the captain at the head of the team
- Joining in with the players for their pre-match kickabout – before structured warm-ups took over – and sending some pea-rollers in at the goalkeeper before he kindly lets one in and the crowd behind the goal cheer their approval
- Going up to the centre circle with the captain for the toss-up, and then being presented with the referee's shiny, low-value coin to keep as a memento before sprinting off to reunite with proud parents on the sideline

There's no joining in warm-ups or collecting coins from the ref these days, but mascots have still been known to make their mark. Though they were given a memorable example of what not to do by five-year-old Chelsea fanatic Jake Nickless, who was mascot for a match with Liverpool in 2005. When opposition captain Steven Gerrard led his team down the steps to the pitch, little Jake called out the Liverpool captain's name and stuck out his hand. When kindly Gerrard went to shake it, cheeky Jake snatched it away and thumbed his nose at him instead. His Chelsea-supporting dad was behind it all, bribing the kid with the offer of five PlayStation 2 games if he dared do it. Jake told the BBC years later, 'My dad said I had to stand out and that's why they dyed my hair blue. The handshake was his plan as well but I told him I was too shy to do it. But when I saw him [Gerrard] in the tunnel it was just instinct.' When the Nickless family found out that Gerrard had mentioned the incident in his autobiography and there was a picture of it in the book, they sent him their copy and he kindly signed it for them and returned it. All's well that ends well – not so much thumbed-nose as thumbs-up.

There have been other examples of mascots not shaking hands with rivals, but often as not it's because they're bemused and overwhelmed by the experience, and normal life hasn't prepared them up until then for the whole handshaking business. But one young mascot who did mean it was a Spurs fan who avoided shaking the hand of Luis Suárez in 2013. Just before he scored a couple of goals for Liverpool in a 5-0 win against her team. The mascot's dad said, 'I said I'd give her £20 to give him the thumb to the nose and the twiddly fingers and it made my day. You can see it was a bit of fun – she laughed and he did too.'

The highest profile mascot in the last few years was brave youngster Bradley Lowery, who tragically died from neuroblastoma, a rare form of cancer, in 2017. In just six precious years of life he'd been mascot for Sunderland, Everton and England and touched the lives of everyone who saw him. None more so than his hero, Jermain Defoe. The two became the best of friends with the striker memorably and movingly pictured on the lad's bed during a hospital visit. Defoe rewarded young Bradley by scoring at Wembley in the England match that took place after he'd led the teams out.

Apart from being a mascot, young fans can also get close to the action by volunteering as ballboys or girls. The most famous one was the Swansea ballboy who held on to the ball rather too long when Chelsea were chasing the game in a Capital One Cup semi-final in 2013. Chelsea's Eden Hazard vigorously tried to get the ball back from under the lad and was sent off for his aggressive actions. The ballboy had rather blown his cover by tweeting before the game that he would be 'needed for timewasting'. It was a bit of a five-minute wonder and Hazard and the ball-keeping ballboy sort of metaphorically kissed and made up when they apologised to each other afterwards.

There was nearly a repeat a year later when Chelsea suspected a ballboy had been unnecessarily slow in returning the ball as Crystal Palace held on to beat them 1-0. Chelsea manager José Mourinho stepped in and told the BBC afterwards, 'The kid was cute and I told him "you do this, one day somebody punches you". We saw what happened with Eden.' It was by no means the last time Mourinho had got involved in a 'chat' with a ballboy and when he was Spurs manager in a match at Southampton he got booked for remonstrating over deliberate time-wasting. But the boot was on the other foot when a quick-thinking ballboy was so fast in getting the ball to Serge Aurier for a throw-in that it led to a Spurs goal. That was in Mourinho's first game in charge of Spurs, a 4-2 win over Olympiacos in the Champions League, and he high-fived and hugged the ballboy. Speaking to BT Sport, Mourinho said, 'I love intelligent ballboys. I was a brilliant ballboy as a kid and this kid was brilliant. He understands the game and he got an assist.' Somehow Mourinho being a brilliant ballboy seems very believable, even if we've only got his word for it.

From one side of the touchline to the other, Billy Koumetio went from Liverpool ballboy to Liverpool player in just a couple of years. He became the club's youngest ever player in the Champions League when he came on as a half-time substitute in a group match with Danish outfit Midtjylland in December 2020. Good old Billy, following in the footsteps of the legendary David Beckham – he was a mascot for Manchester United at West Ham when he was 11. Young Beckham warmed up on the pitch with Bryan Robson and Gordon Strachan and was allowed to sit on the bench for the game before spotting himself on *Match of the Day* that evening. And at least one Premier Division boss was once a ballboy before going on to manage the club – Sheffield United's Chris Wilder did the honours for his boyhood team.

And finally there was a bonus for parents of ballboys at Stoke City as youngsters came home having learned how to wipe up properly. Once they'd retrieved a ball, their job was to dry it thoroughly before handing it to Rory Delap. For years he was the club's long throw expert, hurling the no-longer-wet ball to the far post from way out on the touchline.

25

Our stories: We shall not be moved

ON OUR last morning in Florence during a lovely holiday in Italy, my wife and I agreed we would do separate things. We'd done the galleries, the cathedral, the campanile, the shops on the bridge and some beautiful gardens. She wanted to visit the market to look at leather bags and I wanted to go to Stadio Artemio Franchi, home of Fiorentina. It was summer and no football was on, but I love sport stadiums, in and out of season, and the walk to it was fascinating in itself.

Once there I did a circuit of the outside of the ground and was about to head back to our meeting place in the market when a minibus full of teenage students pulled up. They were heading inside on some sort of tour so I tagged on at the back. Pretty sure I didn't look at all out of place.

We marched down through the stand to the edge of the pitch and started walking round it. They'd been told to go nowhere near the freshly re-seeded precious playing surface but one of the students stepped on to the grass.

All hell broke loose. Someone blew a whistle, stewards and groundsmen appeared, and we were quickly escorted out again. Tour over. It reminded me of a scene in the film *Hard Day's Night* when The Beatles are chucked off a bit of grass and Ringo says, 'Sorry, we hurt your field, Mister.'

What follows is other fans' stories of one of their memories from their football-supporting lives.

Ian Thompstone

For a friend's 40th birthday, his family bought him a ticket to see his favourite team Liverpool play my team Manchester United. It was on 6 December 1997 and they bought me a ticket, too, so I could accompany him.

We drove up to Liverpool and as we parked in one of the side streets a group of children offered to mind my car for 50p. I decided that was cheaper than having scratches repaired, and the transaction was completed.

We went into the ground and found our seats – they were in the middle of the Kop! As a passionate United fan I knew I would have to sit on my hands and keep quiet. Half-time came in at 0-0, but into the second half Andy Cole scored. My first reaction was to stand up and scream 'Yeah!' before reality struck as I realised I was the only person reacting. I took my seat again, kept quiet, and the game continued. Liverpool equalised with a penalty and I was the subject of reasonably friendly abuse. Ten minutes later David Beckham scored and I was up again but this time, over 20 seats to my right, it had got too much for another United fan who was on his feet as well. It was like something from a horror film with a few thousand pairs of eyes on us. United scored again very quickly afterwards with the same reaction from the two of us.

At the end of the game I knew I was being treated as the enemy. Nothing was said or done but if looks could kill I wouldn't be telling this tale.

The trip home was very enjoyable for me but my friend was quiet. A walk to the pub at the end of the journey brightened him up somewhat.

Rob Brydon-Brown

Monday, 27 May 1996, the old Wembley stadium in its full glory; 75,000 fans in for the First Division play-off final. My beloved Crystal Palace v Leicester City. In glorious sunshine me and my mate Paul cheered and roared as Palace went ahead. Then the low of a Leicester equaliser. Extra time loomed and it was a stalemate. With penalties coming up, the worst thing happened as Steve Claridge scored the winner for Leicester in the last minute.

Gutted, we trudged off down Wembley Way to the tube station in total silence. Then Paul said it: 'The Tango Man was fucking epic.' God, how we laughed like two kids until it hurt. At some point in the game, a big, and I mean BIG, bald bloke started running up and down the terrace. He was painted orange head to toe in what looked like an orange nappy. The stewards ran around like something out of *Benny Hill* trying to catch him, with our entire end cheering him on. They finally caught him to a massive round of boos that had the players looking round to see what was happening.

They marched him off and it all settled down. Then a couple of minutes later he'd broken free and the whole thing started again. Huge cheers, theatrical boos, and more *Benny Hill* chases.

I missed football during lockdowns. What we had in place with the TV coverage was mildly entertaining but without fans, it was nothing.

Richard Busby

In my three years as a student in Manchester, Jeff Blythe and I watched a lot of football, almost all of it at Old Trafford or Maine Road. But near the end of our time there we thought it would be a good idea to try and see something in Liverpool.

We planned to see two games – and this was in the day when you could just turn up and pay at the turnstile. First was to see Leeds at Goodison in a cup tie. Great game, my team Leeds won, but I was a bit mouthy afterwards and for the only time in my life we got duffed up.

This didn't put us off, however, and soon afterwards we skived off afternoon lectures to go to Anfield to see Liverpool in the European Cup. Sadly I can't remember who the opponents were. On the train there it began to snow. We walked from the station to the ground as the snow settled. After queuing for a while we got in, found a place on the Kop, and looked forward to the game.

Five minutes before kick-off it was announced that the game was off! I can claim to have been to Anfield, paid my money and never seen a game. I don't have great memories of watching football in Liverpool.

Robert Anthony

I love a football stadium. I've been to nearly all the big ones in this country, and a good few abroad. So I was dying to tick Tottenham's spanking-looking new stadium off my list once it opened in April 2019.

And what a treat it was. It rises majestically but proportionately into the night sky as you approach it, inevitably feeling bigger, better and shinier than the old ground. We walked round the whole of the outside, a lap of honour if you like, delaying the gratification of going in. Staff at the entrances, by the staircases and in the impressively big refreshment facilities, were polite and extremely efficient. Long may that continue and long may there be employment opportunities, albeit part-time ones, for hundreds of local people on matchdays.

Inside the ground, it's everything you'd expect from a modern stadium, and perfect viewing positions from every seat in the house, I assume. It sure lived up to expectations and it was an absolute treat to go there.

On the way back to the underground, we saw a spectacular crash when a pedestrian trying to cross what must have seemed a quiet main road with no cars about was knocked over by a cyclist. Both men ended up on the ground, each blaming the other vociferously for causing the accident. A lot of noise and kerfuffle but no one hurt. A bit like the Spurs defence that night.

David Bryden

I first went to Charlton as a seven-year-old – a 0-0 draw with Newcastle – but too big a crowd to be safe for a little lad so, instead, my father started to accompany me to The Valley on alternate Saturdays to watch Charlton's reserves.

Armed with my autograph book I sought out as many signatures as I could, and Malcolm Allison always patiently signed – over and over – until he began to recognise me every other week.

A year later he said goodbye as he was off to West Ham, but one weekend they were playing at Charlton and there was Malcolm striding out of the corrugated shed that was the Hammers dressing room. 'Hello,' I said, and he remembered me from signing his name in my book so many times. 'Do you want me to collect West Ham's signatures?' he asked. He returned with the whole team signed in and gave me half a crown as well!

In 1980 I bumped into him in a London watering hole the day he was sacked as Manchester City manager and we shared a bottle of champagne. He then moved on to Crystal Palace and each day walked from Norwood Junction station past my office to Selhurst Park and, of course, I contrived to meet him from time to time and chat.

Finally, in 1989, I went to a pre-season match at Fisher Athletic in London's Docklands where he was now manager. As we watched the game, he outlined his grandiose plans for the club to become a league team. He was sacked three months into an unsuccessful season.

I was sorry when he died; to me as a child and an adult, Malcolm Allison was kind, generous with his time, and polite – a gentleman.

Sophie Jones

I can't even remember what the bet was about now as it was a few years ago, but I know I lost. It meant my boyfriend got to pick what we'd do the following Saturday. I was sure he'd choose going to football, and I didn't mind because I enjoyed it, but then he announced it was going to be a double header. A non-league game at lunchtime followed by a quick dash to Southampton, because he'd never been to the St Mary's Stadium. For such a long day I needed extra company, so I asked my best mate if she and her boyfriend would 'like' to join us.

At the non-league match we were able to roam around the terraces to visit the refreshment hut, and we just happened to be in line with a striker scoring the winning goal when he was clearly offside. In fact, we were more in line with him than the linesman was and the goal was allowed to stand.

In the car to Southampton, we discussed how there must be a better way using modern technology to decide such decisions, and how it shouldn't be left to mere human beings. In that Ford Focus that day, we basically devised VAR (you're welcome). But now my boyfriend wishes we hadn't done it. Whenever a forward is given offside by his kneecap or a protruding elbow, he blames himself (well, the other three of us to be specific) for ever thinking such a thing was a good idea.

Paul Joines

My late dad was a ground-hopper and once took me and my brother to Amsterdam as he'd got tickets without telling us to see Ajax play. It was a treat as my brother had just had an operation on his leg to remove excess bone. We loved trains and got the Eurostar to Brussels and then a train on to Amsterdam.

The game went to eight minutes of injury time and we realised we had only 25 minutes to catch the last train back to Brussels. At this point my dad gave my brother's crutches to me to hold and threw him over his shoulder in a fireman's lift to carry him back to the station. We ran through crowds of people and eventually made it back to the station with three minutes to spare. What a sight we must have been and what fun you have going ground-hopping!

Charlie Wright

If someone offered me a free ticket to go and watch my nearest Premier League team, I would check first to see if my local non-league club were at home as I'd sooner go there any day.

I prefer everything about it and I think football is football whatever level you're watching. I also like that it's near where I live, that I'm among people I know – some I even like – and that I feel safe. I always want my team to win but as long as they put in a good shift and look as if they're trying I'm happy whatever the result. I also like to share a bit of a joke with opposing fans, as when all's said and done, that's what it's all about.

One thing I hated was when an opposition manager came up after the game and rudely celebrated a snakey 1-0 win for his team right in front of the home fans. Not the noisy lads behind the goal who'd been singing all game, but the mainly older folk round the side of the pitch who don't go there for that sort of nonsense. I don't know this manager's name but I'd recognise him if he tries to do it again next season. I like a bit of humility in victory, not celebrating like that when all he's done is buy in what was probably a stronger squad because he's got someone rich bankrolling his club.

26

Extra time: It's the final countdown

WAITING IN Sardinia for Italia '90 to start, some England fans took themselves off to an ancient Roman amphitheatre to see a performance of the opera *Aida*. Pete Davies in his terrific book *All Played Out* said, 'One of them came back and complained the intervals were too long.' But he added thoughtfully, 'Would he ever in his life have seen an opera if he hadn't been an England fan, mucking in and making friends in Sardinia?'

Of all the anecdotes and stories in this book, I think that might just be my favourite. This was only a year after the Hillsborough disaster, a few years since Italian fans died at Heysel, hooliganism had done its best to wreck the game in our country, and all the while English clubs were banned from European football. And in Italy itself for the 1990 World Cup, the police were at best tough and intimidating, and English supporters waiting for the games to start were being egged on by a few irresponsible members of the media to get involved in hooliganism or vandalism so they could get pictures to take and stories to write ('Here's a brick for you to throw through that shop window.').

So instead of fans who were smashing up restaurants and picking fights, Davies came across ones who were willing to embrace new cultural experiences. Things they would simply never have thought of trying back home. And isn't that one of the joys of being a football fan? Going to new places, seeing new things, meeting new people, trying a different beer, being out of your comfort zone, but secure that the people around you have got your back if trouble should suddenly appear around a corner?

I set out to write this book about the fun of being a football fan. It was definitely intended to be light-hearted because I knew there was plenty to laugh about and lots of things for us to enjoy. But it's taken me in other directions as well, and I found out more about myself along the way than I'd ever previously considered.

For a start, I've talked about how you pick a club to support – or probably someone older chooses it for you – and they're your team for life. My dad took me to Millwall when I was seven, I took myself there throughout my teenage years, and I loved it and everything about the club. The feeling of belonging, the camaraderie, the shared passion, the impression we were all in it together. Okay, and no one liked us, either. I still have a picture of the Millwall team from that era on display in my garage where, admittedly, nobody other than me ever looks at it. I've been to the New Den and I enjoyed it but I don't support Millwall any more, even though all my life I've gone to watch football.

There are two reasons for that. One, that my career in journalism took me away from Millwall, and when you start reporting on a different football club for a local newspaper you don't half want them to win. It makes writing about them and getting interviews so much easier and more fun. And two, I hated the hooliganism of Millwall 'fans' in the 1980s, like that night at Luton as described earlier in the book. Not that it was just Millwall, it was anyone at any club who wanted to jump on that ridiculous bandwagon. To me, supporters who belonged to firms, went looking for fights and taking on rival fans and police, were a disgrace. They were selfish and ignorant and kept proper supporters away from the games. Imagine introducing your own seven-year-old to a game if they stood a chance of getting hit on the head by a stray bottle or seeing violence take place right in front of them. I knew it was only a minority who used the excuse of a football match to go out and hunt down trouble, though it wasn't just pubs and shops they were demolishing. I'm trying not to be melodramatic, but it was the hopes, dreams and pleasure of millions of others.

I wonder now how a fundamentally decent country allowed this comparatively small number of people to create such dangerous hatred and havoc, destroying the football experience for many of us and ruining the reputation of our country. To read on Facebook the ongoing nostalgia of now middle-aged thugs for those 'good old days' is nauseating.

Thank goodness we live in better times, with safety in and around football more or less assured now, and only the poison of racism left to be eradicated as it continues remorselessly into the 21st century. It's no compensation to state that racism has largely gone underground where tiny minds among a dwindling minority cloak themselves in anonymity to dish out hate-filled abuse on social media. That, of course, makes it – and we've seen this before – a problem for society as a whole to confront, not just football.

Not all the changes and 'improvements' to modern-day football have been plain sailing and straightforward – change is hard for all of us to fully take on board at any time. I get the fact it's sad leaving old grounds we knew and loved, for all their poor, out-of-date facilities and smelly toilets. And there's quite a cost to being a modern-day football fan. Not just mentally, but financially too. A survey worked out that an average Premier League fan will spend nearly £2,000 in a typical season. Mostly on match tickets, travel, TV subscriptions and food and drink, while £23.8m was spent on replica shirts by dedicated fans in the 2019/20 season. Before the pandemic, fans coming from overseas to watch Premier League matches contributed more than £684m to the UK economy in a single year, according to the Office for National Statistics. Visiting fans numbered about 800,000, with Manchester United and Arsenal the most popular destinations.

TV coverage has also impacted enormously on supporters since the Premier League has grown and grown. Preparations for not being able to go to games because of the coronavirus lockdowns began to be unwittingly laid down for us in the previous decade. For a fan who reckoned on seeing all his club's matches, home and away, a new style of fixture list made this impossible. Certainly if public transport was involved.

Matches were rescheduled to suit television, and Arsenal fans wanting to see their team play at Manchester United in the sixth round of the FA Cup in 2015 were furious when it was slotted in for a Monday evening. The last direct train back to London would have meant leaving Old Trafford at half-time – the alternative was a train to Wolverhampton and then dossing down on the platform for half the night to wait for a 5am London connection. A National Express coach left Manchester at midnight, arriving in London at 6.20am. So it was either go by car and drive back, travel on a dedicated supporters' coach, or miss going to the game and watch it on TV. Or, as one Arsenal fan tried, ask the BBC's Gary Lineker for a lift back with him afterwards. 'Just me and 8,999 mates!' he tweeted.

Foreign ownership of clubs raised a few blood pressures, everyone was understandably infuriated about the proposals for a European Super League, which were very quickly spiked, and about VAR when it was introduced in the Premier League. But despite all this, football was ticking along pretty well before coronavirus crept up and then almost immediately overwhelmed us early in 2020. With football, as in life, we'd taken for granted what we had – and only appreciated it properly when we lost it. Basically we were locked out of all football stadiums for well over a year, with the odd reprieve at odd times for a few clubs. We were lucky we could still watch football, albeit at home and on big screens. But if we'd ever wondered what it would be like to go for such a long time without actually going to a match then we all found out.

A football match can be a great piece of art in its own inimitable way. Without sounding pretentious, imagine the *Mona Lisa* or Van Gogh's *Sunflowers* with no backgrounds behind the main subject. They'd still be wonderful, of course, but it wouldn't be the complete picture. Then look at photographs or videos of goals being scored when we had packed stadiums, and see the backcloth of fans rising out of their seats as one, very much part of the whole drama of what's being played out in front of them.

As we know now, football continued to exist without fans, but it's so much better with them, for everyone; the fans themselves, of course, but also for the players and the clubs as well.

Watching a match on TV is no substitute for all the sights, sounds and smells of actually being there. So how long will the cumulative effects of the lockdowns and shut-outs continue to be felt? Weeks? Months? For ever? Certainly, some people drifted away from the game, never to return. Some had got lazier and just couldn't be bothered to make the effort any more. Others felt the game itself had changed from the one they fell in love with. Some older fans were scared to put their health at risk by ever again mixing closely with others in crowded places, having become so accustomed to living their lives at a social distance. And many, many more just couldn't wait to go 'home' again.

The bigger the club the less they rely on gate receipts as a main source of income – at Manchester United, for instance, the figure is about 17 per cent of total revenue. But for smaller clubs, even a few less spectators who were too scared or too indifferent to come to football any more would be a crucial miss.

In November 2020 a time capsule was buried at Liverpool's new training ground and it's due to be opened after 50 years underground. Among the things they'll find wrapped up in it are a pair of manager Jürgen Klopp's glasses, a signed pair of Virgil van Dijk's boots and signed gloves from goalkeeper Alisson. What on earth will football fans in the year 2070 make of those artefacts? And what will football be like then anyway? It's going to be a fascinating, rollicking 50-year journey for us all before we find out the answer to that.

Acknowledgements

THANK YOU to Frances Rickson, Jessica Rickson, Will Rickson and Geoff Rickson for their support, advice, comments, knowledge and suggestions.

Thank you also for their various contributions to Ian Thompstone, Phil Smith, Richard Busby, David Bryden, Neil Thompstone, Ian Scammell, Ken Medwyn, Sophie Jones, Annie Lee, Rob Brydon-Brown, Robert Anthony and Charlie Wright. And thanks to everyone who has ever publicly shared information about being a football fan. That includes newspapers, broadcasters, online contributions through Facebook, Twitter, YouTube, Instagram and more, and the fans themselves.

I am also grateful to Duncan Olner, Graham Hales and all the team at Pitch Publishing for helping to make this book happen.

Bibliography

John Aizlewood, *Playing at Home* (Orion Media, 1998)

Duncan Alexander, *OptaJoe's Football Yearbook 2016* (Century, 2016)

Derick Allsop, *Kicking in the Wind* (Headline Book Publishing, 1997)

Peter Ball and Phil Shaw, *The Umbro Book of Football Quotations* (Stanley Paul, 1993)

David Beckham with Tom Watt, *David Beckham, My Side* (CollinsWillow, 2003)

Jamie Carragher, *The Greatest Games* (Bantam Press, 2020)

Tony Cascarino (with Paul Kimmage), *Full Time. The Secret Life of Tony Cascarino* (Simon & Schuster, 2000)

Jimmy Case, *Hard Case: The Autobiography of Jimmy Case* (John Blake Publishing Ltd, 2014)

Peter Crouch, *How to Be a Footballer* (Ebury Press, 2018)

Pete Davies, *All Played Out* (Heinemann, 1990)

Matt Dickinson, *Bobby Moore: The Man in Full* (Penguin, 2014)

English Football, A Fans' Handbook, 1999/2000 (Rough Guide, 1999)

Rio Ferdinand, *Rio: My Story* (Headline Publishing Group, 2006)

Rick Gekoski, *Staying Up: A Fan Behind the Scenes in the Premiership* (Little, Brown, 1998)

Jimmy Greaves, *My World of Soccer* (The Sportsman's Book Club, 1967)

Duncan Hamilton, *Provided You Don't Kiss Me* (Fourth Estate, 2007)

Nick Hornby, *Fever Pitch* (Gollancz, 1992)

Vinnie Jones, *Vinnie: The Autobiography* (Headline Book Publishing, 1998)

Frank McAvennie, *Scoring: An Expert's Guide* (Canongate Books, 2003)

Paul McGuigan and Paolo Hewitt, *The Greatest Footballer You Never Saw* (Mainstream Publishing, 1997)

Garry Nelson, *Left Foot in the Grave?* (CollinsWillow, 1997)

Opta Football Yearbook 2002/03 (Carlton Books, 2002)

John Boynton Priestley, *The Good Companions* (Heinemann, 1929)

Harry Redknapp and Martin Samuel, *Always Managing: My Autobiography* (Ebury, 2013)

Tony Rickson, *Gooaal: The Joy of Football Celebrations* (Pitch Publishing, 2020)

Ian Ridley, *Floodlit Dreams* (Simon & Schuster, 2006)

Dave Roberts, *The Bromley Boys* (Portico, 2008)

Peter Robinson, *Football Days Classic Football Photographs* (Mitchell Beazley, 2003)

Kevin Sampson, *Extra Time* (Yellow Jersey Press, 1998)

Frank Skinner, *On the Road* (Century, 2008)

John Smith and Dan Trelfer, *Booked! The Gospel According to Our Football Heroes* (Pitch Publishing, 2018)

Jeff Stelling, *England's Worst Footballers* (Orion, 2004)

The Official Football League Yearbook (Facer Books, 1988)

Tony Thornton, *The Club That Wouldn't Die* (Tiger Publications, 1994)

Tony Williams, *The Barclays League Club Directory* (Burlington Publishing, 1991)